RECOVERING
FROM
THE AFFAIR

YOUR GUIDE TO SAVING YOUR MARRIAGE AFTER EMOTIONAL OR PHYSICAL INFIDELITY

By

LEE H. BAUCOM, PH.D.
www.SaveTheMarriage.com

ASPIRE PUBLISHING

COPYRIGHT NOTICE

This book is dedicated to my many clients over the years who now illuminate the path.

CONTENTS

Copyright Notice ii

Introduction 1

Chapter 1: OTHERS HAVE BEEN HERE 7

Chapter 2: ROCKET FUEL OF INFIDELITY 19

Chapter 3: WHY IS SEX SUCH AN ISSUE? 33

Chapter 4: YOUR SPOUSE CHEATED 46

Chapter 5: SO, YOU HAD AN AFFAIR 62

Chapter 6: FORGIVING AFTER INFIDELITY 89

Chapter 7: TRUSTING AFTER INFIDELITY 109

Chapter 8: REBUILDING YOUR MARRIAGE 122

Conclusion: (STARTING POINT FOR YOU) 149

Resources 153

About The Author 154

INTRODUCTION

Let's be honest: this is not a book you ever want to purchase. You didn't buy this book to read for pleasure. It's unlikely that this book will ever be the focus of a book club. You are reading this because you need to be reading it. It is in your hands because you need the information.

This book is designed to help you move through the pain of infidelity and give you the tools needed to rebuild your marriage. Not everyone takes this path. Sometimes infidelity is the end of marriage. But it doesn't have to be.

In fact, that is the reason for this book. I want to provide you with a roadmap of the process. It may not be an easy process, but it is an important process. You have the opportunity to decide the direction of your marriage, starting today. Infidelity may have torn your marriage, but that is not the same as killing your marriage. Only you can make that decision.

I don't know whether you committed infidelity, or suffered infidelity. I don't know if you and your spouse are working on this together, or if you're starting the process by yourself. This book is designed to help you, regardless of your starting point. If you committed infidelity, I will speak frankly to you about how you need to move forward in order to get beyond it. If you suffered infidelity, I will tell you the tasks you need to take to move forward. If you are starting this process on your own, you will find information to help you begin the process. If you both have decided to work on the marriage, you will find resources and tools for each of you individually and both of you as a couple.

Infidelity, whether emotional or physical, tears at the fabric of marriage. When it happens, it can feel as if there are no alternatives then to get away from the marriage. The pain is emotional and physical. Regardless of whether you committed infidelity or suffered infidelity, you face a painful reality: your marriage vows are broken. Your ego has likely taken a hit. The hurt goes deep.

But I know there is a spark of hope within you. How do I know it's there? You opened this book. If somebody put this book in your hands, they had hope; but it also took hope for you to open it. If you had no hope, you would've tossed it aside. If you found this book, you were searching for a solution. Searching for a solution reveals the spark of hope.

If you are wondering whether it is even truly possible to restore a relationship after infidelity, let me assure you it is. I've seen it time and time again. In most cultural and religious traditions, infidelity opens the option of ending a marriage. But those traditions don't require it. The choice is up to you. I would suggest you lean into the hope of restoring your marriage and move towards the healing of it.

I promise to be honest with you throughout this book. I won't pull punches. We won't be delving into the deep subconscious, searching for pathology in your personalities, though. We will discuss what went wrong in your relationship. We will discuss what fuels an affair. We will discuss the damage done and the actions needed to restore the relationship. My goal is to provide you with practical information. My goal is not to provide a good armchair read, but an actionable roadmap back to a great marriage.

I recognize that at this point, you may be undecided on the outcome of your marriage. That's fine. I get that. And I would be surprised if you were 100% committed to this process. But if you're reading, I also know that you are at least open to the process. So, we will move forward with this process, which can restore your marriage. This is not an intellectual endeavor, but an endeavor of action. You can't heal a marriage simply by reading about it. It will require action. From both of you. While one of you can start the process, eventually it requires both of you. If both partners are not on-board right now, we will be moving in that direction throughout this book.

One caveat: there is a type of relationship I do not recommend working on—an abusive marriage. Let me make it clear that my information is designed to help couples who have the potential of a healthy relationship. I do not condone being a part of an abusive relationship. If you are being abused, don't focus your energy on saving the relationship. Focus your energy on being safe. Your personal safety is more important than restoring the marriage. If you are being abused, please contact the National Domestic Violence Hotline (1-800-799-7233) right now.

If you are still reading, I assume your relationship is free of abuse. I assume you have at least some measure of desire to restore your marriage. And I assume there has been infidelity in your relationship, whether emotional or physical.

I also assume we are now joining together, as a team, to work toward a loving and respectful marriage which you will treasure and protect. I assume we will be working through the disconnection and the lack of boundaries, the hallmarks of relationships ruptured by infidelity. I also recognize that this is not an easy process. It can be painful. It can be tiring. It can be frustrating. But, it will be rewarding.

Let's take a quick look at where we are headed in this book, and then, let's jump in and work to save and restore your relationship.

In the first section, we will take a look at why sex becomes such an issue in relationships (since affairs are sexualized, in content and/or actions). We will also look at the "Rocket Fuel" of affairs. Why do they burn so hot? Why does it feel so powerful? This helps us understand the emotional power and force of an affair – and why it can have lingering effects for all concerned.

In the second section, we will look at tasks for each person. There is a section on what you need to do if you had the affair. These are specific actions that can help you and your spouse move beyond the affair and get back into a place of integrity. There is a section for what is needed from the person who suffered the affair. Again, these are specific actions that help to restore the relationship. (If you find yourself saying, "Why should I have to do anything?" understand that all have to take responsibility. Life is not particularly about what is "fair," but what is helpful and healing.)

In the final section, we turn to the issues of trust and forgiveness. They really go hand-in-hand. In this section, we will discuss re-establishing trust and the process of forgiveness, so the marriage can be strong and resilient.

One note: You will notice that I do not distinguish a "type" of affair. Other authors suggest there can be any number of types of affairs. In those theories, how you address a specific affair depends upon the kind it is.

First, I am not convinced that the "types" of affairs really change the healing process. My reason being there is a consistent pattern underneath it all: a disconnected marriage that does not have clear boundaries.

Second, I am not focused on getting an affair to end. I am focused on how to move beyond the affair to save and restore the marriage. The path to healing has much less to do with discovering the "type" of an affair, and much more to do with how you reconnect and heal.

And finally, I watch many people spend an inordinate amount of time dissecting and diagnosing the affair. This fixation often keeps the healing process from progressing. In the end, I am solely focused on getting to the place you have a marriage you cherish and protect.

If you are on-board with that, let's get started!

**As a reader of this book, I want to provide you with an extra bonus I didn't include in this book. In the bonus, I collected some very common questions that come up for people as they move through this process. Then, I answer them. Resources are provided for each of you.

Go here for your Bonus:
http://savethemarriage.com/affair-bonus

Chapter 1

OTHERS HAVE BEEN HERE

Infidelity is an absolute kick in the gut. If your spouse was unfaithful, you know this. The images (actual or imagined) flash in your mind, the unknowns haunt you, and the hurt you feel is as physical as it is psychological. If you were unfaithful, you may just now be starting to understand the pain caused by your actions.

You think you will never get over this.

You will.

You fear your marriage cannot be saved.

It can.

You are not sure if you will ever let your spouse touch you again, or if you can ever trust your spouse again.

You can.

It will take time. And healing. And changes.

If you committed adultery, you may be at a different point. You may not be sure whether you want to stay or go. You may even wonder if that other person is "the one for you." The feelings you had, the rush of emotions and connection, can leave you confused about your marriage, love, and what you want out of life.

Or you may deeply regret what happened, and wish you had never gone down that path. You may wish you could rewrite history and undo that first step toward infidelity. You may wonder if your spouse will ever love you again, want to be touched by you, or ever trust you.

You may feel all of these things simultaneously.

Infidelity is a major upheaval in a committed relationship. It breaks the bond of trust and invades the safety of that relationship. In a marriage, this is even more so. After all, during your wedding vows, you likely said some variation of "forsaking all others."

The statistics on infidelity are a bit murky. It turns out that people are not overly willing to reveal acts of infidelity, even anonymously, to researchers. More than that, some people are confused and unsure about whether or not it really was infidelity.

Some studies have shown that roughly 22% of men and 14% of women commit emotional or physical infidelity in their marriage. Other statistics have found that upwards of 40% of marriages have suffered some level of infidelity. But as I stated, accurate statistics are a bit hard to dig up.

What is important to know is that many other people have been exactly where you are. Some lost their relationship. But many went on to have a great marriage – sometimes even stronger than it was before the affair (remember, something led to it – we will get to that shortly).

Statistics are big numbers about lots of people. They don't matter a bit to you. If you have a deadly disease that kills 95%, and there are 5 out of 100 people who live – you want to be in that latter group! The only fact that matters is what happens to YOU, not what the statistics say.

So, what are the chances of saving your marriage? The answer is less about statistics and more about the choices and actions of both you and your spouse.

I knew from his first contact with me that George had been involved in an affair. Then Susan and George came into my office together. As they sat in my office, I learned the affair was fairly extensive. George had become involved with an assistant at the office. It started with "innocent" banter over coffee. That led to lunch. Which led to dinners. Which led to texts, sexting, and sex.

Susan had been a bit suspicious. George mentioned this colleague more and more frequently – and suddenly stopped mentioning her. He had more and more "work commitments" and "projects." He seemed more distracted, disinterested, and short tempered.

But when pressed, George swore that nothing was going on, all was fine, work was stressful, and it would pass.

It didn't pass.

Susan was busy, though, with her own work, the kids, and her involvement in the community. She trusted George.

Then one night the toilet backed up. Their child watched as the half-bath off the kitchen didn't flush down. After two more flush attempts, the water was coming over the rim; she finally called out for help.

George leaped from the couch and headed to help – leaving his phone behind. Susan saw an image come across his lock screen and felt the blood leave her head. She thought she might faint.

The picture of an almost-naked young woman included the text, "I want you."

Susan was shaking. She felt she might throw up.

George had changed his passcode, so Susan had no way to see anything more.

When George had taken care of the toilet, he came back to finish their movie . . . only to find Susan in tears, angry, shaking, and holding his phone.

"What are you doing?" Susan demanded. George was caught off guard, but knew he had been caught. He pretended not to know.

Susan's tone changed. "Don't. Lie. To. Me." She spat the words and stared him down.

George didn't come clean at first (big, but common, mistake). He played it down: "I don't know what that was about," "Just a little innocent joke," "She's crazy," "Okay, we talked, but nothing more," "Yes, we made out, but that is all," "Okay, we had sex, but just once."

Susan demanded the truth. Admittedly, by this point, she had no idea what that meant and when it was being spoken.

What happened? How had Susan and George ended up at this place? George was not a bad guy. He and Susan held the same values. George loved his family. He had sworn this could not happen to THEM, to their marriage. But it did.

How did this happen?

Infidelity has two common traits: lack of connection and lack of boundaries.

To say it differently, a well-connected marriage where both people enforce clear boundaries in dealing with other people is safe from infidelity.

A marriage where the connection between the couple has waned, and where boundaries are either not known or not enforced, is just waiting for the right opportunity (or wrong, depending on your viewpoint) for an affair – emotional or physical – to occur.

Does that mean that every disconnected marriage where the boundaries are not clear will suffer from infidelity? No. The opportunity and circumstance that lead to it also have to be present.

But a disconnected relationship with poor boundaries is at risk. It is a highly combustible situation waiting for a spark.

And what a spark infidelity can be! (We will look at the combustibility from disconnection, and how an affair becomes so charged, in a later chapter.)

For the person involved in an affair, the first barrier we must face is denial. Denial is not so much about pretending an affair did not happen (if it was/is physical), but of the damage done.

Let's take a look at three different levels to this denial.

The human mind is quite an interesting thing. It has the capacity to talk its way into just about anything. In fact, neuroscientists have strongly established that decisions are first made on an emotional basis. We then rationalize the reasons for the decision to make it "make sense."

More than that, we all like to think the better of ourselves. Most of us believe we are fine, upstanding citizens who are moral and respectable.

Most people will state they do not believe an affair is the best choice for a relationship. And yet, many people have affairs. This causes the unfaithful individual to rationalize why that action was acceptable.

One way was to see it as something different. In other words, they rationalize the behavior.

Here are some of those rationalizations:

- "It was only about sex."
- "The other person came on to me, and I was: drunk, tired, high, hurt, frustrated, lonely, etc." (Choose the reason)
- "My spouse didn't seem to care about me, so I don't know why my spouse would care about the affair."

I remember, years ago, I was meeting with a couple. They had married out of an affair. The current (3rd) wife was the prior affair partner. His wife before had been an affair partner while married to his first wife. And now, he was involved in another affair.

My client wanted to break off his affair and stay in his current marriage. His wife was not so sure. She turned to me and said, "I thought we had something different, that I was not just another affair."

He turned to her and said, "You weren't just a fling! I married you. It was different."

At that moment, she turned on him and said, "I was your third affair that I know of. You have now had two since. You have an issue."

I was silently in agreement.

Imagine my surprise when he turned to me to say, "I'm not a philanderer, you know."

It took a second for me to respond, "Sir, you are the definition of a philanderer. This means there have been at least five affairs."

He paused and said what we all want to believe about ourselves: "I'm a good person with strong morals."

We all want to believe ourselves to be moral people. And yet we all make mistakes – moral mistakes – at various times.

So we rationalize. Here are a few:

1) "It wasn't a big deal."

Let me be very clear: infidelity, either emotional or physical, is a very big deal. It is a painful rupture of the trust necessary to sustain a marriage. It is utter rejection to the spouse who suffered the affair. And it causes a shift on the part of the person who had the affair.

It is a big deal.

I'll give you the fact that in the process of falling into the infidelity, the person committing it may have told him/herself, "This isn't a big deal. It's just a date/email/text/kiss/sex/etc." But it is a big deal.

2) "It wasn't cheating."

This is yet another rationalization. The person recasts the behavior differently than seeing it as infidelity. This is more easily done in cases of emotional infidelity than physical infidelity.

Sometimes, people will rationalize that the other person, when it is an emotional affair, is just a really good friend. Maybe even their best friend. They may claim the flirting is "just us having fun, nothing serious."

They share more and more intimate areas of their lives – even critiquing their spouse and talking about their marriage issues – but say it is "just friends sharing."

Many times, when the relationship turns physical, they may say, "We just kissed. We only made out." A little further along, they may say, "It wasn't sex. It was just oral sex."

There is a gray area of relating that can be a bit unclear for some people. Friends do share with each other. And I do believe it possible to have friends that are the same sex as your spouse. But, how much sharing, and what type is acceptable, must be agreed upon between the spouses.

When boundaries are clear and spouses stay connected, these friendships can be kept safe.

When emotional content comes into the relationship, the friendship can become fraught with dangers.

One early clear sign of danger is when you are talking to this friend about things you do not bring up with your spouse – including problems with your marriage.

A second danger is when you begin to hide encounters and conversations from your spouse. We humans tend to hide things for which we feel some guilt or shame. Hiding is an indicator that something is hitting our guilt-factor.

When you are taking any energy out of the marriage that should be shared in the marriage, you are cheating the relationship of energy. Early on, it may not quite be infidelity. But people only have so much energy.

If the energy is drained away from the marriage, the marriage suffers. More than that, wherever we focus our energy grows stronger.

3) "It's not my fault."

Again, we all like to think of ourselves as moral and upstanding. This means we all have a tendency to shift responsibility away from ourselves and toward someone/something else.

Two "someones" often get the blame in an affair: the spouse and the other person.

It is easier for us to see the shortcomings of others than to look in the mirror and see our own. Therefore, people easily see the infidelity as a result of someone else's actions.

People often blame their spouse for being disconnected, not attending to their needs, not being available, not being "sexy" or exciting, gaining weight, growing old, having been a bad choice, etc., etc., etc.

Social scientists have well established the tendency to "blame the victim," and this is the rationalization that does just that.

More than a few sessions with a fractured couple have started with "If you had/hadn't done ___, I never would have ___."

Let's be clear: each of us is 100% responsible for the actions we take.

But could a stated reason be true?

Yes.

A marriage may be disconnected. A spouse may be unavailable. We all age. And sometimes, life isn't particularly exciting.

But this is not an "If/Then" equation. Those can be true, and there could still have been a choice of fidelity.

Sometimes, it is the OP (Other Person) who gets the blame. They showed too much attention, they kept on messaging, they undressed in the office, they took advantage of a drunken state. The reasons go on. But again, this is simply shifting responsibility for personal actions to someone else.

Taking action is entirely the responsibility of the person who took action.

Wow, that was a harsh section, wasn't it?

Let's go over it one more time: It is impossible to put a marriage back together until the actuality of the affair is accepted, responsibility for the affair is accepted, and it is accepted that cheating IS a big deal.

Denial keeps the process stuck. Accepting responsibility helps shift to the healing that can happen.

It is also the path back to having a great marriage. Two people taking 100% responsibility for their own actions, leaning into the marriage relationship, can create a world-class marriage.

Which leads us to the spouse who suffered the affair. We will discuss this in more detail in a later chapter, but to be clear on this point: you have to take responsibility for your role in a disconnected marriage.

The spouse who suffered the affair cannot be blamed for the actions of the affair. However, that is different than taking responsibility for your role in the state of the marriage before the affair.

My guess is your marriage was not where it needed to be. It may have been stuck for many reasons. Perhaps there were typical relationship fears. Maybe you thought your marriage was just "on pause" during a certain phase in life (actually, there is no pause button in marriage). Possibly, hurt and anger had contaminated the relationship (they are really the same thing) and led the relationship to deep disconnection.

Whatever the reasons for the disconnected relationship, both people have room to take responsibility.

Oh, and by the way, only by taking responsibility will the relationship get to the place it needs to be. Don't brush this step off. A connected relationship requires two people to accept responsibility to move toward more and more connection.

We will talk more about this later, but when you think about it, responsibility has nothing to do with blame. Blame is about pointing a finger at something. Responsibility is about claiming and choosing your response. Your "ability to respond" is your response-ability. And step one of this process is reclaiming responsibility for where things have been and (more importantly) where you want your marriage to go.

Two people, accepting full responsibility for their own actions and working together to build a strong marriage, are unstoppable. Ready to move in that direction?

Allow me to reiterate that I do not distinguish between "types" of affairs as other authors suggest. Some have created a rather complex taxonomy of affairs.

I don't make those distinctions.

As I stated earlier, I am not convinced the "type" of affair changes the healing process. The consistent pattern underneath it all remains a disconnected marriage that does not have clear boundaries.

I also stated previously that I am not focused on getting an affair to end and I don't think labeling the "type" of affair really changes much about that process. (By the time you read this, the affair has likely already wound down or stopped.) I am focused on how to move beyond the affair to save and restore the marriage.

And finally, I mentioned that I watch many people spend an inordinate amount of time dissecting and diagnosing the affair. This fixation often keeps the healing process stuck. All that to say, I am about getting to the place where you have a marriage you cherish and protect.

The process I use involves understanding why affairs are so powerful and choosing the actions necessary to rebuild from there.

If you want more training on why there is no "Pause Button" in a marriage, go here:

http://savethemarriage.com/nopause

Chapter 2

ROCKET FUEL OF INFIDELITY

———⁓———

Let's talk about what fuels the affair relationship. Why is it so intense? Why does it burn so hot? Because it is such an intense relationship, many are left to wonder whether it is even possible to avoid or avert infidelity. The answer is absolutely. But the bigger question it raises is why it happens. I've discussed elsewhere in this book about my belief that when there's a lack of connection, it puts a relationship at risk, and when there are lack of boundaries around the relationship, there's even a higher level of risk. Lack of connection and boundaries creates a powder keg of potential for infidelity in a marriage.

It's important to understand why infidelity becomes so intense. Sometimes it becomes very confusing for both the people who are involved in the infidelity and for the person who is hurt by that infidelity. To clarify, I'm talking about any infidelity, any affair, whether it's emotional or physical. But, understand that the physical aspect certainly adds fuel to that fire. It's like rocket fuel that burns so heavy, so hot, and is so explosive. That's why it is difficult for us to understand what's going on. This chapter is less about action and more about understanding.

I do want to make a little disclaimer here. Emotional infidelity is difficult to clearly define. Often, a person is sure their spouse is having an emotional affair, and the spouse refuses to see it. There is a substantial gray area of emotional infidelity. But this information still applies. Just recognize it's a little harder to get that understanding across, given the denial mechanisms that happen in an emotional affair (we will discuss that later in this chapter).

When we talk about a physical affair, it is usually very clear because there's physical contact; the line from emotional infidelity to physical infidelity is crossed. It changes when the relationship goes from sharing one's inner life to sharing a physical connection of some sort. So even if it's "just making out," there is a physical level of infidelity – leading all the way to the point of sexual intercourse.

Let's face it, any romantic physical contact is headed towards sexual contact. While some couples stop at kissing or making out or some other contact, never getting to intercourse, they have still crossed a line. What makes it confusing for people is defining that line. I want to draw that line today, the line that goes from an emotional connection to a physical connection. It is simply the point when there is romantic physical contact. But recognize that this energy, the power around an affair, happens in both physical and emotional infidelity.

I remember one couple that came in my office. They couldn't figure out why he was unable to break away from the affair. He wanted so badly to end that relationship, and yet he found himself drawn back in – to texts, to phone calls, to elicit meetings. It was as if he could not get away from some powerful pull. Which all points back to the power of an affair relationship burning on that "rocket fuel."

As I've talked to couple after couple, I've discovered there is a common theme of what fuels infidelity. I will use an acronym so you can easily remember what is fueling this affair: **F.A.L.S.E**. It's FALSE because it's not real, but it feels that way. Here's why:

F is for Fantasy

One of the key pieces of an affair is the fact it is based in a fantasy life. It's not based in reality. It's not based on raising children, getting up in the morning, getting ready for work, and struggling through the day. It doesn't include seeing each other at the worst moments when people are exhausted and tired, sick and down. It's built in a fantasy life of getting all cleaned up, getting dressed, of meeting somewhere interesting, creating a sort of fantasy around the other person. In fact, most of the time it very much is a fantasy about the other person. People will rationalize this, claiming they do really know that other person; but they're not seeing them in any other context than this fantasy arrangement.

When that happens, people create a story through imagination. We humans have some core human needs. Sometimes, those needs compete. For example, we like to have something we can count on, yet we also like variety. Those two human forces, liking sameness and liking variety, are present at the same time. The infidelity fantasy often steps in when someone feels like there's not a lot of variety in life. That can be very alluring, even addicting. You see your spouse when your spouse is not cleaned up, and when your spouse has bad breath, and when your spouse is sick, and when the kids are grumpy, and when the job is not going well. That's one little story to tell about "sameness." Then there's this other person and the fantasy life. It is often about romantic settings and dinners, sexual excitement, and both people being a bit more careful about appearances.

So, the F is this strong layer of fantasy that exists in the affair relationship. It's not about knowing someone in day-to-day life; it's about living in a fantasy world. If you watch what happens on reality TV shows about dating and courtship, you'll notice that producers put those couples in fantasy places, knowing that fantasy draws out passion. These interesting places and beautiful surroundings are out of our normal life. This accelerates the level of attraction between two people, which leads to the second part of the equation. It also raises the adrenaline load and thus, the adrenaline attraction.

A is for Adrenaline

Whenever we talk about infatuation, adrenaline is always a part of that. So the A in FALSE is adrenaline attraction. That adrenaline attraction is always based on that excitement. And the excitement drives us towards something. Adrenaline, as you probably are well aware, is a very addictive substance that we create in our own body. That same charge you watch adrenaline junkies go after is the same adrenaline that fuels the fire of affairs. Adrenaline is always the beginning point of a relationship. When we're in an infatuation level, it's always about adrenaline.

I want to draw one crucial distinction about adrenaline. It always has a level of fear to it. Whether that fear is of getting caught, or whether it's because you're breaking your values and your norms, or whether it's based on the fear of losing that other person. There is a fear level that fuels it.

That's the opposite of what happens when we are in love, when we switch from our adrenaline attraction to an endorphin attraction. Adrenaline attraction is always based on getting that jolt of excitement, feeling that charge. Whenever we're away, we're pining for that other person, pining for that punch of adrenaline, and probably worried a little bit that the other person is possibly finding someone else attractive. That's what happens in the early stages of any relationship. We get that charge out of being with them, and we get another charge as we wonder what's going on with them when we're apart. That's true in an affair.

But when we love, we switch over to the endorphin system in our body. Endorphins make us feel good, but without fear. Endorphins are triggered when we do loving things. Adrenaline is triggered when we're going after something, grabbing something, getting that charge. Endorphins are activated when we're giving our love. This is one of the clear distinctions between a loving, long-lasting relationship, and an affair. Adrenaline fuels our fantasy world.

L is for Lostness

Often, the affair relationship is based on a feeling of "lostness." That's the L in FALSE. Many times an affair erupts when somebody is feeling particularly lost. Maybe the marital relationship is not clicking the way they want it to, or the connection is not there. Maybe their job is no longer satisfying, and they're not sure what to do next. Maybe the kids are reaching a new stage in life, and they're not sure what the next chapter brings. Roles may be changing anywhere in life, leading to the feeling of being lost.

You might treat the feeling of "lostness" by finding another person and disappearing into the relationship. If things are not going well in an area of life – if somebody is feeling lost and stuck – and then the affair comes along, it can distract from that mental pain. It doesn't mean that it was "meant to be," and it doesn't mean that it's "the perfect relationship," or any other rationalizations. It's just a way some people try to treat the feeling of being lost.

Remember that "lost" is one of the central feelings of a midlife crisis. In a midlife crisis, people feel lost and don't know what to do next, don't know where to go, don't know how to find meaning. They're trying to find something that will soothe that feeling of "lostness" or emptiness.

An affair is an attempt to find that something, and not in a healthy way. It does create a distraction from the lost feeling.

The lostness of life often finds its salve in an affair in very inappropriate ways. But that's also part of what fuels it.

S is for Secrecy

The "S" is also a powerful fuel for an affair: "secrecy." In fact, secrecy is one of the biggest fuels in an affair. Whenever you can't tell people what you're doing, you probably shouldn't be doing it. That's typically true with an affair. People don't usually announce they're having an affair, that they're cheating on their spouse. (At least not in the early stages – maybe they do later in the rationalizing process.) And that secrecy heaps fuel on the other pieces of the equation. The secrecy creates more of a fantasy life, and the secrecy strengthens that adrenaline charge. When you have to keep secrets, there's an exciting level of fear to it.

The secrecy grows in the extent people go to hide things. There may even be hidden phones and apps to hide communication. In recent years, I've noticed many creative ways people use technology to escape being noticed. That fuels the secrecy, which fuels the affair.

Often, when an affair is finally discovered, it begins to fall apart on its own because that secrecy is punctured. It takes away something of the belief, the self-rationalization that this is hurting nobody, that it's okay. It takes away the energy of having to be secretive, joined together by the deception. And suddenly, it all comes crashing down when the spouse learns about it.

There's a song you might remember from the 1980's titled, "Secret Lover." It is probably my all-time least favorite song. In fact, when it comes on, I turn off the radio. I quit listening to one station because they played it too often. I complained to another station and asked them to take it off their playlist. All it does is glorify infidelity. The song makes it seem as if that "secret lover" thing is okay. It gives approval to having to put up with day-to-day life by having this little "secret lover" on the side.

Truth is, secrecy eats away at all other relationships. The person begins to work very hard to hold onto their secrets, covering them up with more and more lies. As we all know, once you tell a lie, it spins out to lie after lie after lie to cover that first lie. Suddenly you're lost in the dishonesty. You're lost in the secrecy that comes with that dishonesty. And pretty soon that spirals into this powerful link between two people acting dishonestly, caught in a web of lies.

When people are keeping secrets together, it bonds them in ways that are very dangerous, at least outside of the boundaries of a real relationship. I say a "real relationship" because the majority of affairs do not last. The majority of affairs fall apart at some point, if for no other reason than the people involved in the affair realize there's a dishonesty to the relationship and they can't even trust the person with whom they're cheating. Because they know that person would cheat. They often begin to self-implode as one or the other recognizes the dishonesty that's involved.

I once had a couple in my office. They were together because they had both cheated on their spouses, and then married each other. Here they were once again in trouble. The man had once again cheated. The woman made a comment to me that she should have known that if he cheated on his first wife, he would cheat on her –if he could be dishonest once, he could potentially do it again. She knew that because she had been a part of the relationship that came out of that dishonesty, that secrecy. But she had rationalized that they were the right match. It's very rare that an affair puts two people together into a healthy relationship because it starts in such an unhealthy place.

In fact, as many people as have proclaimed to me that they finally found their "true love," it has never panned out. You rarely find someone healthily in this process of infidelity. The health of the relationship is already at risk. The secrecy just fuels the relationship, throwing gas on the flame, giving it more and more energy.

E is for Ego

And that leads us to the last piece, the ego, the E in FALSE. The ego really fans the flames because the ego is about "what I want." Somebody is getting an ego charge out of the fact that somebody wants them so much. This is yet another huge part of what fuels the affair, this feeling of being wanted. It often comes, as I said earlier, out of the disconnection in the marital relationship, leading to an Achilles heel, a wound that's not getting treated in the relationship. In the disconnected marriage, there is a bruised ego from feeling unwanted, which may lead to looking elsewhere for an ego boost.

Affairs often develop at nodal events in life, turning points or major transitions. For instance, one risk point is when a couple is expecting, or has a young child, because the attention of the couple becomes focused on that child. That can be an ego bruise.

Or when a child starts school or goes off to college, there can be an ego bruise of a loss in the parenting role. There is an ego bruise in any role loss – it leaves someone feeling "less than." Or when there's a job problem: the job is not going well, is ending, or somebody's stuck in a job. There can be an ego bruise, leaving somebody vulnerable to an ego stroke, a way of feeling better about things.

But love is not about ego. Love is about caring and attending to the other person, protecting the relationship. An affair is about the ego and getting what you want. Even the acts of what look like love that happen in infidelity really are about maintaining and keeping that person around to make sure that it's an ego stroke, that it continues to fuel that pattern.

There you have them, the fuels of infidelity. Fantasy, Adrenaline attraction, the Lost feeling, the Secrecy that's built up, and the Ego looking for attention. Pretty clear, but not very pretty. Sometimes, this is a painful realization, even confronting. And many people insist this is NOT the case in their situation. But with a little time and distance, the way we humans fool ourselves and rationalize our behavior becomes a bit clearer. The intensity of the fuel can sometimes keep us from wanting to see the dynamics in a situation. As the fuel burns out, the factors become clearer.

What these factors also tell you is what it's not about. It's really not about that other person. It's not about the person with whom somebody's having an affair. That person becomes an object and often a projection (or fantasy) of what a person wants. The affair partners imagine certain traits in each other. They begin to take subconscious or unconscious material and try to make that person what they want them to be, even if it's not at all true. The person becomes an object of infatuation and projection, a fantasy. By the way, that brings up the point that it's not really about love. It truly is about infatuation. To be clear, all relationships start in infatuation. And some relationships make it to love. That is rarely the outcome, though, of an affair.

The problem with an affair is the infatuation is rooted in such dishonesty and secrecy and adrenaline, it rarely has any chance of moving beyond that. The relationship is based on dishonesty, which begins to eat away at the foundations of that relationship. Very few affairs can make it very long in real life because they already have the danger points built into them at the foundation.

Also, it's not about life. The escapism that happens in infidelity is incredible. People go to great lengths to sneak around and see each other; that's just not real, day-to-day life. That's a fantasy life which is not sustainable, and in the end, not particularly fulfilling. It might meet a need here or there, but it can't meet all of the needs that are necessary for a relationship. That wrecks the affair relationship.

It's also not about honesty. No matter how many times I've heard two people involved in infidelity tell me they are 100% honest with each other, I know the relationship is not rooted in honesty. With only rare exceptions, affairs happen outside of the affair partners' values. This points us back to what the problem is: human wiring is always for connection. We desperately want to be connected to another person in deep, intimate ways. When we're looking for that connection, sometimes the wires get crossed and therefore when we connect, it's inappropriate.

Instead of wanting to admit to that, it often leads to rationalization of emotions and actions. Somehow you've got to make the relationship acceptable.

It's well established in psychology (and in the marketing world) that people first make a non-rational, emotional, primitive decision, and then they back it up with reasons to justify it. We always believe we're making a reasoned decision, but it's always ruled by that non-rational, emotional, primitive choice.

Let me give you a couple of simple examples. Look at what you're driving. Unless you're driving the most basic car that will get you from here to there – and even a car might be a step up from what is really necessary – a non-rational decision was made. What you need is the most basic level of transportation that will get you effectively from place to place. If you have more than that, you have made an emotional decision. The only thing a vehicle needs to do is to get from point A to point B. Everything else is all about wants --not needs, but wants and justifications.

Any time a car is purchased with more than the very basic capacity of travel, a non-rational decision was made and probably justified. I include my car in that. When I look at it, I admit I didn't get the most basic model. I didn't get everything, but I didn't get the most basic model, and so I made a non-rational decision. And I rationalized it. I "needed the room," and leather is easier to clean. And when we travel, satellite radio would be nice. But was it a need or a want?

Let's use another example. This was pointed out to me at a conference. The speaker said, "Look down at your wrist at the watch that's on your arm. Is it a Timex? Because if it's not a cheap $12 Timex, you made a non-rational decision in your purchase. All you need a watch to do is tell time. That's all it needs to do." When I look at my wrist, I see my dive watch. It will tell me the water temperature, how deep I've gone, how long I've been underwater, and lots of other cool facts, all on a large face that shows the world I am wearing a dive watch.

But, the fact is, when I dive I carry a dive computer, which tells me how long I've been under, how long I can stay down, what the water temperature is, and all the other things my watch does (and then some). When I bought my watch, I made an emotional decision and then backed it up with the rationalization that I need to know those things when I'm diving. "It's a back-up for my computer," I told myself.

What it really does is remind me of my love of scuba diving. It tells others about my love for diving. In that way, it's an irrational decision. It's an emotional decision because it's tying me to something else. That's the nature of humans. We make irrational decisions, or non-rational decisions, that are often based on some primitive emotion, and then we spend our time justifying that choice.

This is true in affairs. Affairs happen based on non-rational decisions (and the desire to have sex with somebody else is, by the way, a primitive decision) and then we spend our time trying to justify it. We try to find rational reasons for the affair instead of recognizing that we've allowed our emotive, primitive side to take over the sensible side. We've allowed that place of fantasy, of adrenaline, of maybe feeling lost, holding onto secrets, and needing an ego stroke to lead us to a place of cheating. And then we try to make sense of it.

If you're the person who has suffered the affair, recognize that it is not about you. If you are comparing yourself to this other person, stop. It is not about comparisons because it's not about the other person. That other person functions as an object, as a projection of your spouse's imagination and other subconscious desires.

If you're having an affair, recognize that you have been caught up in the process. And that process rarely goes to a healthy place when it starts with a values violation. Very few people can tell me (in a rational moment) that affairs make sense and that affairs are okay. Yet many, many people commit affairs. Many people who are good and decent spend their time living in a fantasy, driven by adrenaline because they're trying to deal with that lost feeling. Then they create secrets that lead further down that road, all while trying to get an ego boost.

That's a quick and painful look in the mirror or look through the window, whether you're having an affair or whether you are dealing with a spouse having an affair.

Almost always, rocket fuel burns out; it burns hot, but it burns out. Hopefully, this knowledge will give you guidance for moving forward. The question is not really whether it will burn out, but what gets scorched along the way.

None of what you have learned will immediately remove the hurt and pain, or the confusion and excitement, of an affair. But it does give you a path through the process of recognizing the affair for what it is: an escape, a non-rational/emotional decision, and a blaze of a relationship that is untenable and unsustainable at least 99.9% of the time. Chances are very good this is true in your case, too.

Chapter 3

WHY IS SEX SUCH AN ISSUE?

―――――――――⌁―――――――――

According to surveys, people say they left a marriage because of only a few major issues, sex being one of them. The five top issues are money, kids, religion, in-laws, and sex. The only one that is specifically in order is money; it is actually the number one stated reason for leaving. The others (kids, religion, in-laws, and sex) are in no particular order. Sex is usually listed somewhere between number 2 and number 4 as a major reason people leave a marriage. Which raises the question: Why is it such a big issue?

We're in a culture that is awash in sexuality. It is the major focus of media and much of advertising. We are surrounded by sex and sexuality daily. It captivates us, yet we have very little real information about it – just tantalizing images meant to excite us into consuming.

A sexualized media surrounds us, but what we don't know is what's "normal." Are we getting enough sex? Are we getting too much sex? Are we doing it right? Are we doing it wrong? Sex is still such a taboo subject that we don't know. Even though imagery surrounds us, sensible discussions are in short supply. It's not like our parents told us what was going on with them. At least, most of the time they didn't give us a clear message about what they were doing. Sometimes we weren't even aware that our parents were involved sexually (and just like our kids, we would rather not think about it).

We have all these mixed messages that come at us: from being told early on how we should or should not react and respond – and yet being subtly encouraged in other directions – to being surrounded by peers that often gave misinformation, to having religion play a role in our beliefs about it. Maybe we received some sex-education in school that really didn't answer many of those questions at all. All the while, we're trying to figure out what it's all about.

We have very few clear studies that show us anything useful. When researchers do surveys, they get a wide range of answers about whether people *feel* like they're having sex too much or too little. It has no correlation, based on the general population, of whether people are actually having sex very often or not often at all. I've talked with some people who felt like they were having way more than enough sex, and it was once a year. I've also talked to couples that were having sex every single day and didn't feel like it was enough. Many times, one spouse is satisfied with frequency and the other is not. And then there are issues tied into attraction. Does a person have "chemistry" with their spouse? One of the things that I often hear is, "My spouse said, 'I love you, but I'm not in love with you'." In other words, that feeling, that passion, is just not there anymore. Which makes it even more confusing.

My dear grandmother was incredibly open with her discussions and left me with lots of good lessons in life. She once told me, "Chemistry is not really a big deal." She paused for a minute, and she said, "Unless it's not there." When the attraction, the chemistry, the passion is there, it's just a non-issue. When everything is going okay, it's not anything big; but when it's not there, it begins to be a dominant, driving force in a couple's struggles.

Why? Well, we all have multiple layers to our self-esteem. We have several different ways we understand ourselves. One of those layers may be our appearance, whether we feel good about how we look, or how athletic or not athletic we are – our performance layer. Then there's our work self-esteem, how we feel about what we do. Then there are other questions, like, "How are we as friends? How are we as parents?"

And there's also our sexual self-esteem. That's one of the tenderest areas, the most vulnerable place for people to talk about. Our sexual self-esteem has so many components, so many little places along the way where we struggle with understanding, "Am I okay sexually? Am I accepted sexually? Seen as desirable?"

Sometimes, different experiences in life may have damaged this sexual self-esteem (bad experiences, shaming moments, confusions, and rejections). That often carries over to married life. It doesn't suddenly go away just because we marry. People are still self-conscious about it, which can make it tough to have meaningful conversations about it with a spouse.

And there's another layer. There's this fantasy that somehow when you're married, you'll have sexual harmony. The fantasy is in believing everything is going to go just fine and that everything is going to fit together. Here's the problem: We all have different preferences, including how *often* we want to have sex and *how* we want to have sex. Not only that, but there is an ebb-and-flow to it. Two people with two different ebbs-and-flows and two different sets of preferences should not be surprised that sometimes getting together can be very difficult.

One of the times we can feel most rejected is when we're out of sync with our sexuality and our partner. Let's say that one wants to have sex and the other doesn't. Both people are probably going to end up feeling a little wounded: one person's going to feel rejected, and the other's going to feel pressured. At its best, couples find the places where they fit together (and I mean that metaphorically and physically), but there may be times when it doesn't quite click, when it doesn't quite come together. Suddenly that sexual self-esteem is a little bit wounded.

More than once, I've had couples come and tell me very similar stories where one of them was saying, "Well, I wanted to have sex that night and my spouse, once again, didn't want to have sex." The other spouse responded, "I had no idea you were interested! How would I have known? You didn't say anything; you just cuddled up against me." Because of that fragile sexual self-esteem, people have a difficult time being open about what is wanted, what is needed. This is even true (and perhaps especially true) when we're in the protective relationship of marriage. Where we should be more open, we actually often end up being even more closed down.

And so, sex ends up being a very loaded subject for all of us, even in marriage. Marriage should be a place where there is a greater ease of intimacy, yet it often ends up being one more place of struggle in a relationship.

Consider for a moment how vulnerable sex is. At its best, you're talking about two people who can't be any more physically close. There is no other time when we are that physically vulnerable with somebody. You're completely connected with this other person – literally physically connected. There are no other times when you are encompassing each other in that way. There's a vulnerability that we often underestimate, and we often miss how powerful it is in how it shapes us and our relationship. Our limbic system understands this, and this is where we start our discussion on why sex is so powerful in a relationship.

The limbic system is the midbrain. You have this very primitive "lizard brain" (the deepest layer of your brain which is all about survival), which, in terms of sex, is all about, "Can I get that person pregnant, or can I get pregnant?" It's the biomechanical part of how our genes get carried to the next generation. We have that lizard brain that's all about making sure the species survives and keeping the genes in the gene pool. That's all it's about: mating, mating, and more mating.

Then you've got this other piece layered above the reptilian brain. It's more about the emotions (the limbic brain). And above that is the thinking/reasoning piece, the neo-cortex, which has all these thoughts and is processing a "logical" approach, critiquing the self. But the limbic system is all about connection.

When a couple is engaged in sex, the limbic system takes over at that moment. Not when they're trying to figure out what the other person wants (neo-cortex), but when they're engaged sexually. I'm not just talking about intercourse. I'm talking about a sexual act of vulnerability. At that point, their limbic systems end up syncing. Studies show that there is such a thing called HRV, the Heart Rate Variability. This is not just the heart rate of how many beats, but it's the spacing of the beats, and how those beats look, how the shape of the beat changes.

When a couple is having sex, their HRV's begin to sync up and match. They are connecting in ways that are far deeper than their verbal skills are capable of. Some people reduce it to, "Oh, it's just about sex." It's not just about sex. One of the myths we carry around with us is that it's possible to *just* have sex. It's really not; it's not possible to *just* have sex. A bonding happens in the act of sex.

When the Bible talks about someone having sex, the Hebrew text uses the term "to know." I find that to be an interesting term for an ancient culture. It indicates the truth that when people have sex, they learn something not learned any other way. They have a connection with each other. When people say, "Oh, that was just sex," I don't buy it. This is especially true in marriage; there is a deep bonding connection from the sexual relationship. Which is why it's so painful when things go awry, why it's so difficult, and why we get into these arguments and heated discussions.

In case you are wondering, there are clearly some male/female differences – I'm referring to the biology aspect. Having sex, for a woman, can mean bringing another life into the world in a way that men struggle to fully understand. Even if there is protection in place, or even if there is no way for that to happen, there is still a subconscious attribution to this risk for women that is hard for many men to understand. Men are wired with a drive to have sex. So, you see, nature's way of continuing generations also creates a difference in approaching sex.

There can also be competing psychological needs. For a man, there's often a need for feeling competent. How does this play out when he has a difficult time arousing his spouse or performing sexually? It begins to eat away at his feeling of competence, which is why it can be such a battlefield. And why, often, when a man feels like he's not capable of satisfying his spouse, the issue looms larger and larger.

Women have a need for feeling closeness, to feel connected and protected. To be clear, I'm talking in generalities; there are differences from individual to individual. When a woman is driven by that feeling of closeness, and a man is trying to prove his competence, those two desires (closeness and competence) don't necessarily go together, and they can end up causing arguments. That's where we find strains in the relationship.

Then there are also some stereotypes that get in our way. I've heard so many times, "He just wants sex," and, "She doesn't like sex," to know that those are stereotypes that we somehow reinforce. When I talk to men in private, I have not had one man say, "I just want sex. That's all I want. I just want to get off." Yet, I've heard woman after woman accuse the man of that. When I talk to women alone, they tell me how desperately they want that kind of connection, that depth in their relationship. Yet, when I talk with men, they tell me how their spouse doesn't like sex.

It's not about sex, yet somehow it begins to be a tug of war. The accusations come out when there is a struggle.

Our society provides lots of mixed messages. Men see that if you're not able to perform sexually, pop a pill. From the women's perspective, there are a lot of books that say, "Well, what the man needs to do is take care of the house, and clean things up, and then you'll be rested – and then you will want to have sex." In the end, you can't use an outside source to make it work. A pill certainly doesn't fix the relational issues behind sex. It may work on an erection, but it doesn't work to fix the relational issues behind it.

Not only that, but we also have pretty clear evidence that the rate of sex doesn't go up very much when the man takes on more household tasks. It doesn't solve the relational issues. It may for that night, if suddenly, the man takes on putting the kids to bed, getting a bath together, and all that. We call that "being romantic." When it's the norm, it doesn't change the rates. In fact, some studies have pointed to an interesting fact that the more egalitarian the home is, the less the couple has sex. We have these ideas that we fix these things externally, and we miss the fact that there may be a relational aspect that we need to look at.

What is that relational aspect? That sex truly is a connection when it's treated that way. It can be just about getting off. But, if it's only about getting off, masturbation does that. And we know that is not satisfying for most people in a way that sexual intimacy is; the connection is really what we're after. Right now,

I'm setting aside the issues of sex addiction, where it is only about getting the "fix." Let's be very clear: we are all going to get a dopamine load in sexual intimacy. It releases those great oxytocin hormones that are all about bonding. Yet, in the end, let's think about how that helps increase our level of connection with our spouse.

I can't tell you how many times over the years I've had a couple come in and say, "We just don't have time for sex. There's simply no time for it. How are we going to work it into our life?" As a way of doing a little reality check, I'll say, "Hey, let me ask you a question. Did you watch TV last night?" because the vast majority of the country did. If they say, "Well, no, not last night," I'll ask, "Well, how about the night before, or how about three nights ago? In the last four nights, have you watched TV?" Generally speaking, they have. To which I'll then follow up, "How long did you watch TV?" Usually, it's between half an hour and four hours.

Here's the truth about typical marital sex: fifteen minutes to half an hour is how long most couples take to have sex. We have this fantasy in the back of our heads that says, "Oh, gosh. It's going to have to be all night long." That gets in our way. Instead, we should say, "You know what? Prioritizing is important. I can sit here and watch TV and be brain dead, or I could be intimate with my spouse, and still be fairly brain dead while letting my body take over." Let's just take away that excuse. It's not about time; it's about priority.

Another popular mindset is, "I'm not in the mood. I'm not feeling enough connection." Thinking this way misses the fact that if we move in that direction, if we move towards each other in physical ways, the "mood" will arrive. In physical ways, we actually *are* building the connection. We get into chicken-and-egg arguments about whether we start with connection that leads to sex, or sex that leads to connection. The answer is "yes, both." We can do both, and we don't have to say, "I would prefer to be connected before I have sex," or to say, "I prefer to have sex before I'm connected." Connection can lead to sex; sex can lead to connection.

If someone says, "Hey, I want to have sex with you," if you are in a respected, respectful relationship (and marriage should be both), a quick translation is, "I want to connect with you." We get stuck in this rigmarole of trying to tease out who wants what, and all we end up doing is falling back into stereotypes and unnecessary dichotomies.

The priority is really connecting. So, it may be more useful to say, "We are going to work on the connection. We are going to work to be connected. If we're disconnected, maybe this is a way of connecting."

Biological differences do complicate in one area. I've noticed over the years that women vastly underestimate what it's like for men to experience buildup — the feeling of buildup, of wanting release not just through masturbation, but through connection with a spouse. It can go from desire to frustration to anger to resentment.

What I also understand from women, (and again, I'm speaking as a male – I've never been a woman) is that men's needs can make a woman feel like an object and that it's only about the sex. That can feel like being reduced to one element of existence.

We're multidimensional. We're biological. We're spiritual. We're emotional. We're thoughtful. Many different pieces interlock in ways we never fully understand, but we cannot separate one piece from the others. We are built in ways that are sexual.

As we relate to each other, any or all of these dimensions can come into play. Including that sexual attraction piece. On some level, attraction, or "chemistry," floats around. This is true in marital relationships and other relationships. That's why we have boundaries that we place around the marriage. We are basically saying, "It's not that I will never be attracted to somebody else, it's that I choose to never take any action based on that attraction; I'm going to filter my attraction towards my spouse."

When we nurture our attraction and our connection with our spouse, it tends to grow; when we neglect it, it tends to wither. Our choice is, "Am I going to keep that as a priority? Am I going to recognize that this isn't just some sexual thing, this isn't just some physical thing, that there's something else deeper here?" Sex is deeply physical. It's also deeply spiritual. It's also deeply connected. We tend to underestimate that. When someone is in a bad place, they tend to agree with that – on either side of the equation.

Might I suggest for a moment that we suspend all of these bombardments of what this all means to us and say, "Is this about connection? About how we can connect with each other physically, in a vulnerable way, which isn't possible in any other way? Is this about the spiritual, where we get to ecstasy?" Because it is a basic loss of control. You can't have an orgasm unless you lose muscular control of your body. Your muscles have to take over at some point. Some have noted that this is akin to ecstasy in spiritual practice. Can we bring in that piece of it? Most of all, can we recognize the fact that this is a way to connection?

Which leads me to ask: Are we willing to make the physical level of our relationship, a top priority? It's too easy to let other priorities get in the way, to say, "Well if it happens, it happens." In the busy-ness of life, unless you make it a priority, it will not happen.

Secondly, after you decide to make it a priority, you must decide, "I am not going to believe the stereotypes. I'm not going to simply look at my spouse and accuse my spouse of some stereotype. It is likely unfair and untrue. Can I see this as our connecting, as a way of building the connection?" It's both – a way of connecting *and* a way of expressing connection.

What if you decide, "The priority is us connecting"? Is there a connection that overarches your relationship, which is beyond whether you feel extremely connected right now, but based on your willingness to be connected? The dance of "I'll connect when I feel connected" between a couple gets them in trouble. But they can choose to step back and say, "Overall, we have this connection that we can share. And, it can amplify our relationship."

Sex is an issue in a relationship because it is often used as a way to connection and a yardstick of connection. It is both biological release and emotional connection. It is both spiritual and base. We have beliefs and thoughts from childhood and societal norms that can keep us confused.

Yet in a marriage, sex can be a deeply connecting and deeply connected glue. When it is present, issues can disappear. And when it is missing, hurts can be deep. How do you decide to prioritize together?

Three Notes:

1. Sex should feel safe for both people. If sex is physically uncomfortable, talk to a health professional to get to the bottom of it and understand the reasons. If sex is frightening, a therapist can be helpful in getting to the roots of that issue.

2. Sometimes, intercourse is not possible for couples. That does not mean being sexual is off the table. Our culture has made intercourse the "actual sex," but sex is a wide range of connecting. There are many ways to be sexual when intercourse is not possible.

3. In no way am I implying that someone should be or feel forced into sex. Coercion is not part of a loving relationship, sexually or otherwise. There is a difference in deciding to be more sexual with each other and being coerced into sex.

(To be clear, I have grossly simplified some very complex issues that may or may not show up for individuals – and have not covered every layer. My task is not the socio/psycho/biology of sex, but a path to a satisfying marriage.)

Chapter 4

YOUR SPOUSE CHEATED

---~---

Start Here if your Spouse is Having/Had an Affair

We don't have a clear idea of how often affairs happen; different studies show very different results. According to these studies, somewhere between 30-60 percent of people involve themselves in affairs. That's a huge difference in numbers. The reason for this discrepancy is the difficulty we have in defining an affair, especially when you include emotional affairs, and people's unwillingness to talk about them. While 30 percent is likely too conservative, many feel that 60 percent is too high. Therefore, we aren't quite sure exactly what percentage of people have affairs.

More importantly, statistics don't matter. What matters most is what's going on with you. Statistics only apply to a large group of people. Your feelings and experiences are what happen to you. But, my guess is you're here because this does apply to you. If infidelity has not happened in your marriage, you may want to be clear about how to protect your marriage. More than likely, you are reading this because infidelity has either happened or you suspect it has happened.

Let's talk a little bit about what we mean by "affair." The problem is in how we define it. If you say to someone, "Have you cheated in your relationship?" you may get the response, "What do you mean by cheated?" With physical affairs, there's a wide range of behaviors which cause some people to say, yes, they had an affair, and others to say, no, they did not have an affair. Some spouses say if you kissed someone, if you held hands, then it's a physical affair. Others say, no, it has to be sex.

Then we get into the whole question of what kind of sex. That's part of why it's so difficult to get our hands around (and I use that facetiously) what we mean by a physical affair, much less an emotional affair. Let's talk about a broader definition. I would like to suggest that when we're talking about an affair, what we're really talking about is behavior that is inappropriate for the boundaries of a relationship. Something that somehow should be kept within a relationship has spread outside of that relationship.

Here's the tricky part: often, when people are moving outside of what is expected in a relationship, they begin to justify what they're doing. They talk about the emotional affair and say, "Oh, no, it's just friendship. It's just someone I share information with."

That's partly why it's so difficult to get to the bottom of infidelity: there is a difficulty with definition and an issue with personal acceptance.

Let's use this as a broad definition: an affair is something that violates the expectations of a spouse in a marriage with someone outside of the marriage. Now, that does raise the question of whether or not those expectations are understood. To be clear, the spouse does not have to know of the expectation to be breaking it and committing infidelity. Let's talk about that as a violation of the expectations within a relationship. Physically, does it violate what is expected from a physical relationship between a married couple? Do they say that it violates that? In an emotional way, does it violate that? I believe we all have a somewhat finite amount of emotional energy that we're going to invest. If I'm investing that emotional energy over there, I'm not investing over here. It's one place or the other. That's why the emotional infractions damage the marriage.

If there is emotional energy that should be shared within the marital relationship and it's being shared outside the marital relationship – in other words, that emotional energy is going to someone else – then I would say there is emotional infidelity going on. Whether the person who is committing it admits to it or not is a different matter. But I would say, at that point, an inappropriate relationship is forming and invading the marriage. One of the key elements, one way you can look at an emotional affair and see the danger, is how secretive it becomes and if the information that's being exchanged ought to only be shared between the married couple.

If somebody is confiding in someone else outside of the marriage about their emotional life and not confiding in their spouse, they are definitely taking energy away from the relationship and putting it elsewhere. This is very dangerous because it's moving energy outside of the bounds of the marital relationship. It only takes a certain level of slips and mistakes along the way for somebody to fall into an affair. I rarely find people who purposely set out to have an affair. Those who do fall into a different category, which I discuss in another chapter.

For the moment, let's just assume there are basically two types of affairs that are really addictions to either relationships or sex. The addicted person is going out for their next fix. Very generally speaking, we find that men have an addiction to sex, the physical part.

Again, very generally, for women, it is more of an addiction to the relationship. The fix they're getting comes from the relating part. Notice that women can be involved in a physical relationship for the relational connection, of which sex is a part, as opposed to men who are often there for the physical connection, of which the emotions just happen to be a part.

That's generally speaking. It's not always the case, but it often is when an addictive nature is involved. One of the ways we know about the addictive element is from the serial nature presented. People who are addicted to sex or relationships are always upping the ante, trying to find more, trying to get more out of it, because when we're talking about addictions, we're talking about that dopamine load in the brain. At some point, the brain becomes accustomed to a certain level, and it takes more of the addiction to get the same charge.

Let's set those types of affairs aside, because when you find that somebody is dealing with an addiction, they must deal with the addictive part first, not the relational part. They will need to deal with the relational part at some point, but they must first treat the addiction.

Let's examine what is more commonly true in affairs: they happen for two reasons. One is that there is disconnection between the couple. They are not emotionally feeding each other in ways that meet their emotional needs. And secondly, there are not enough boundaries in the relationship. Both of those have to happen at the same time for an affair to have room to develop.

Couples that are disconnected but have strong boundaries to protect themselves are not likely to fall into this trap.

A couple that is very connected, yet without boundaries, is often going to be okay. But there is always a danger to the relationship because sometimes you can be unguarded, a little careless, and find yourself in a compromised situation without realizing it.

Basically, most affairs happen due to a disconnection in a relationship without boundaries in place, with one last ingredient added in: opportunity. Whether the person is seeking connection, or they just happen to find themselves in a vulnerable place and connect, there has to be an opportunity that develops.

The biggest parts that have control over the couple are how they nurture their connection and how boundaries are set for the relationship. Here's the problem: Not many couples realize how important this is. Not many couples talk about the boundaries of their relationship before they get married.

When I work with couples before they get married, that's one of my big questions. What are the boundaries you have in your relationship? In other words, what makes you feel safe and protected in the relationship? What are the situations that you will or will not allow yourself to be in? For instance, is it okay to "Friend" an ex-boyfriend or girlfriend on Facebook? Is it okay to text an ex-boyfriend or girlfriend? Is it okay to have communication with someone outside of your relationship? Is it okay to go to dinner with someone of the opposite sex when nobody else is around? Is it okay to have meetings behind closed doors with someone of the opposite sex? There are lots of ways you can think about these boundaries in practical ways. What do we need to do to protect our relationship?

Then there's the emotional connectedness. Most couples find that the connection ebbs and flows in any relationship. There are times when we feel more connected and less connected to each other. That's just the natural rhythm of relating.

Couples who stay focused on maintaining the connection – really building that connection – will notice there are times when it ebbs and flows, and yet, they'll find themselves on the upper side of it more often than the lower side. Couples who are not conscious of connection, who are not intentional about building it, find that it wanes more often, that life gets in the way. Perhaps they become parents and start focusing on the kids, and the marital relationship takes a backseat in the family dynamics. Or work gets in the way, or volunteering gets in the way – the list goes on and on of all of the things that can keep us away from each other and disconnected if we are not intentional. That's the backdrop of what happens in an affair. It has to have: (a) a lack of connection, (b) a lack of boundaries to protect it, and then (c) the one that is always around us, opportunity.

We're always surrounded by opportunity. A few weeks ago, I attended a conference. I was watching the people after-hours. What worried me most is the amount of opportunity available for people traveling: being in a foreign city, being in the same vicinity with someone who may share the same kind of passions and interests in life. Suddenly, connections are easy to grow when people are not careful. That's part of the society we live in; opportunities arise where it's easier to find someone with similar traits and similar interests whom we were not aware of before our marriage. That doesn't mean that they're the right person for us, but we fool ourselves. What we realize now is that our brain has that deep, primitive place of wiring, and it's looking for connection. As humans, we are built for that connection. When it's not met, we begin to look for places to find it.

Part of that is in our sexual makeup, our DNA. The fact that there can be chemistry and connection is in our wiring. So we protect it ahead of time. To be clear, this is not a justification for why infidelity happens. It's an understanding of why we're at risk if we do not set the boundaries and we do not focus on the connection.

For you, you're likely reading this because it's too late for this speech. Infidelity has already happened. What I'm giving you now is an understanding of where it came from. Later we're going to talk about what to do. But one of the things I would suggest, right now, is that you begin to understand where this is coming from by looking back on where you missed the boats of connection and boundaries. How was the marriage at risk? Then you can begin to understand the roots of the problem.

At this point, I want to state one fact very clearly: If there has been an affair, the person who had the affair is one hundred percent responsible for having not protected the relationship. One hundred percent. Sole responsibility for the actions of the affair is on the person who committed the affair.

That said, both people are responsible for having been in a disconnected relationship. How do you get beyond an affair? You must understand that there was a prelude to it. And second, you must understand that if you stay stuck, you'll be caught in something that perpetuates itself. When we're disconnected, and there's an affair, we tend to disconnect further, which only gives justification to whoever is acting out to act out further. It's not rational, it doesn't make sense, but it's what we keep telling ourselves.

Let's talk a bit about some things to do now. Number one is you need to make the request for the relationship to end. How do you make that request? Here's my formula for requesting someone to stop a relationship. If you have discovered it and they don't know you know about it, start with, "I know about this relationship. I don't need you to deny it or confirm it." That's the first part. You know; you don't need a denial or confirmation. If you simply suspect but don't know, that's different. We are now talking about when you have evidence. You know that something inappropriate is happening. You may even say, "I don't know the extent of this relationship, but I know it is invading our marriage." Part number two is, "Please stop." It's a request. "Please stop that relationship." If necessary, you can define the relationship further.

Then you say, "I'm not going to check on you about this. I am just asking you to stop." Number one is "I know." Number two is "Please stop." Number three is "I'm not going to check." Number four is "I'm asking you stop." Then you wrap it up with a final statement, "There's no need for you to reply or respond or tell me anything else. I leave it up to you to decide what to do."

This formula for confrontation is important for one simple reason: you remain focused and calm. Often, when somebody starts a confrontation, they're angry, they're hurt. They initiate the confrontation defensively, and it ends up being a debate. They argue over what is an emotional affair, what is a physical affair, why is the person justifying. They get so wrapped up in arguing those points they never get to the place of saying, "This is my boundary."

Let's go through that one more time: "I know about this relationship. Please stop the affair. I'm not going to check, but I am requesting you stop. There's no need for you to reply. I just ask that you end the inappropriate relationship."

1) I know. 2) Please stop. 3) I'm not going to check. (By the way, when you say you're not going to check, you're not going to check. We'll get to that in just a minute.) *4) I ask that you stop the relationship. 5) There's no need to reply to what I'm asking.*

Then you remove yourself from that situation. This is not the time for debate. This is the time to confront, state that it's not up for debate, and say it needs to end.

This raises the question of what comes next. Some people ask me, "Should I give them an ultimatum or not?" Here's what is meant by an ultimatum: "If you do not stop the affair, you have to get out. If you do not stop the affair, our relationship is over." That's the ultimatum.

Many people give an ultimatum, which backs them into a corner. Perhaps, at that moment, they do want to end the relationship, and they hope the ultimatum forces that ending. If you haven't made an ultimatum, but are thinking about it, here are a couple of considerations. First, do you think your spouse will actually leave? Second, if the affair were to continue, even for a short time, is it a relationship-ender for you? If you think your spouse might leave, you may decide to not make that ultimatum. If you still want to work on the relationship, even if the affair is not instantly ended, you may not want to make that ultimatum.

A confrontation, with or without an ultimatum, is pretty powerful. Remember, an affair is a fantasy life. When you bring it to their attention, you stomp all over the fantasy – and that's exactly what you want to do. You want to confront from a point of strength, not begging and pleading. That's why I have structured the confrontation to be simple and direct. If you do it the way I laid out, you're doing it from a place of power. That's much better than the endless arguments and debates about something over which you really have no control.

An ultimatum can be a very powerful place if you think it will catch the other person's attention. If you don't, recognize that making an ultimatum may end the relationship. If you're willing to take that risk, then you can still make the ultimatum.

Another question people ask is, "Do I confront the other person?" Generally, I say, yes. You can confront if you can do it calmly, and if you can make a flat request. By flat request, I am referring to both tone and words. The tone needs to be neutral as if you are talking to a neighbor about the weather or the blue sky. You need to speak in words, not insults; no shaming or cursing. You want to confront with a sense of power, not desperation. You can say to the person, "You are having an inappropriate relationship with my spouse. I would ask that you respect the boundaries of our relationship. We are married. I request that you respect that relationship, and you stop having any contact with my spouse."

You want to do it calmly because you don't want to add fuel to the emotional fire. You don't want to have these two "lovers" suddenly thrust together by your anger so that they can say, "See, look at how crazy this person is. This is why we deserve each other." They will use the confrontation as further justification unless you can confront both of them flatly and calmly. "You need to stop. I expect you to abide by the boundaries of our relationship." That is a flat statement, strongly stated. It's neutral.

Sometimes a spouse finds that the other person did not know they existed, having been lied to, just like the spouse is lied to. When you confront them, suddenly they say, "I don't want anything to do with this."

Think how brave you come across when you do it calmly. This other person must look you in the eye or hear you on the phone. They know they're guilty, yet they see you are completely calm and confident as you tell them their relationship needs to end. That is power.

And that's why this often works. At a very minimum, what you are doing is keeping them from playing their head games –

"It's us against the world. We're so made for each other. We're so special. Our love is special." – all the fantasy stuff that's fueled by an affair which is, by the way, not true. I don't know how many times I've had people say to me after they've finally broken off a relationship, "I don't know what I saw in that person. I got caught up in it." It has happened enough for me to know that what's driving the relationship is not love. It's adrenaline. Those are two very different places in the brain: love and adrenaline. As I've discussed before, there is an endorphin love, and there is an adrenaline love. Endorphin love is long-lasting love. It's about "how can I show you my love?" Adrenaline love is "how can I get my thrills?" It's adrenaline driven; it's not really about the other person.

An affair is driven by adrenaline. The adrenaline is going to wear away, and when it does, the relationship often naturally collapses, like a flame cut off from its fuel. You don't want to give fuel to the adrenaline. You want to take the fuel away. You want to take away that fantasy by confronting each person involved, calmly and directly. Generally speaking, if you can confront calmly and with a flat request, I suggest you do it. If you cannot do it because of your own emotions, then don't. It will only get out of hand and add fuel to their fire – and probably backfire.

There are a few things you should not do in the midst of an affair.

Number one is you should not compare yourself with whomever they're having an affair. It's really not about the other person. It's about your spouse.

An affair is a selfish place to be. It's not about this great person they found. Over the years, I have often had the spouse say, "I don't understand why they're with this other person. They're not as attractive as me. They're not as smart as me. They're not ____ (fill in the blank)." It has little to do with the other person. It has nothing to do with you. It has everything to do with your spouse trying to find something out there. Don't ever compare yourself. This is not a beauty, talent, money, or any other kind of competition. Don't fall into the comparison trap.

Number two is don't believe the fantasy. They're going to talk about how they have found their true love, and it is forever, and all those other things. Don't believe the fantasy. In fact, as much as possible, you want to break the fantasy. Part of what fuels that fantasy is the secrecy. That's why you confront. Breaking the secrecy breaks the fantasy. That's where we want to be.

Number three is don't believe you can't recover. When you get stuck in that place where you believe there's no way to recover from this, then you miss the fact that countless couples do recover. In fact, more couples keep their marriage together after an affair than those that didn't have an affair. To be clear, there are couples who can't make it past an affair. But plenty do. You may hear that staying married after an affair is impossible. That's not true. You can recover, and you can actually have a stronger relationship. You now know that your relationship is more vulnerable than you believed, and you will do something to fix it. That's how you get past it. You realize there was a vulnerability and weakness you did not see before, fix it, and restore your relationship.

It requires you to make a decision. "We will find a way around this. We will work to get beyond it. We will build a relationship that we can treasure forever." That's when you break the belief that you can't recover. Don't believe you can't recover.

Number four is don't refuse to forgive. We have the mistaken notion that forgiveness is about this other person whom we're forgiving. It's not. Forgiveness is for you. Forgiveness is so you do not have to carry the hurt and pain forward.

Forgiveness is not the same as saying, "Okay, I'm all in. We'll just go with whatever happened. Everything's okay. Que sera, sera." That's not forgiveness. Forgiveness is saying, "I am going to see this differently because I do not want to carry this around the rest of my life. I want to be relieved of it." You may choose to forgive, and still choose not to stay in the relationship. Those are two different decisions.

Generally, people say, "I'm not going to forgive you because then you'll be off the hook." Guess what? They were never on that hook that you thought they were on. When people don't forgive, the other person may say, "Okay, that's fine. If you're not going to forgive me, I'm moving on because I'm not going to be held in this place."

Choose instead to forgive. Not necessarily to rebuild the relationship, but so you don't have to drag the bitterness around. Don't refuse to forgive – choose to forgive so you can move forward, and then decide what to do about the relationship.

Number five is don't play detective. It's very tempting to play detective. You're going to want to look at emails, Facebook, phone records, and countless other places. Don't do it.

Playing detective does not get you any closer to working on the relationship; it only gets you stuck in an adversarial role. Don't play. Once you know that an affair has happened and once you've confronted, leave it at that. Let your spouse decide what they're going to do, and don't get caught up in detective work. The more you do it, the more you nurture that place in you that needs to do it. It does not help you, and it rarely helps the relationship.

That doesn't mean you have to ignore all the signs, just don't go digging for them. Don't install a new GPS location system. If you know it has happened, you have all the information you need at that point. Down the road, your spouse may choose to win back your trust. To do that, they're going to have to be transparent. But right now, in the midst of it, don't get caught playing detective.

Finally, number six is don't threaten. Don't threaten your spouse, or the other person, with anything. Don't tell them you're going to tell their employer, or the police, or your attorney, or the other spouse, or anyone else. Don't threaten. Threats come from a place of weakness. Tell them what you expect and stop there. Often, we get pulled into threat mode when we are caught in a "fight-or-flight" place, and that does not bode well for recovering from an affair. Don't get into that threatening mode. Be the "bigger person." Raise the standard of what you expect of yourself, and keep moving forward.

At this point, you know the "Dos and Don'ts" of confronting and dealing with the reality of an affair. We have discussed how to confront both the spouse and the affair partner. We discussed some things to avoid. And I have suggested that the process back is really about forgiveness and connection.

A later chapter will cover the forgiveness process and the connecting process. The start of that process is the ending of the affair. This chapter is for you to do what you can to start that process.

Chapter 5

SO, YOU HAD AN AFFAIR

———⁓———

Start Here If You Are The One Who Had The Affair

In this chapter, we look at what the person who committed the affair needs to do in order to repair the hurt and damage caused by it. But my goal is not just about "damage repair," it is about personal transformation. One is a bandage. The other is about healing.

Many times, when someone is searching for information on saving a marriage after the affair, they are the one who "suffered" the affair. They didn't commit infidelity but are the spouse of the one who cheated. But many people say, "That's great, but what if you're the one who did have the affair?" So, let's discuss it from that side. Let's talk about what you need to do if you are the one who committed adultery. This is straight talk. There are no punches pulled because my desire is to help you get back to your marriage.

You are not in the same marriage you had previously. Let's face it, there is obviously some vulnerability in your relationship which created the current situation. We want to get to a new place, a new marriage that will sustain itself, that will sustain you and your spouse. That's the reason for this book.

After spending about a quarter of a century in the office speaking with couples, I think I've seen every reaction possible when someone admits, "I had an affair." I remember having one couple come in, and when the husband revealed it (I wasn't aware of it myself), his wife tore through my office throwing books, pushing things over, completely enraged about the affair.

I really thought that we were going to have to call in some help. She began to calm down when she realized that what she was destroying was not her husband's property, but mine.

At the other end is another couple. I remember it was on Valentine's Day; it will always stand out in my mind. I had been working with the man for some time.

(By the way, just because these two examples are men, it doesn't mean everybody who has an affair is a man. Let's face it, whoever that man is with is often a woman, right? I'm just using these as two examples.)

Having talked with him, I knew about his affair; it had been a one-night stand. But it made him think that maybe his marriage just wasn't meant to be. That was his justification for his behavior. (We'll talk about that in just a bit.)

He was in my office that Valentine's Day. His wife was sitting at the other end of the couch. I asked, "Is there anything else you want to say?" I was not trying to get him to tell her about the affair; I was simply asking if there was anything else he wanted to share.

Well, he did. He revealed the affair – to my disbelief, because he had told me that he had no intention of talking about that affair.

We had talked about this in an earlier session. He had shared that he didn't know what he wanted to do about the marriage, but he knew he didn't want to talk about the affair. (We'll talk about whether you tell or don't tell in just a little while. I'm going to tell you some reasons why you might go either way.)

So there we were, on Valentine's Day, and he turns to her and tells her that he had an affair. What I expected to happen didn't. She sat there quietly, blinked a few times, and said, "Oh. Oh. I guess I can't really blame you." Now, she could have blamed him, but what she realized is what is true for the predominant number of affairs that happen: They were disconnected as a couple.

There are a few important pieces to unpack in that statement. Generally, affairs come from a disconnected marriage that is then not protected (disconnection and lack of boundaries).

And she knew the disconnected part – how disconnected they had been as a couple. She was not surprised that the relationship was also not protected. It was not something they had ever discussed, and she had seen other times when each of them played a little close to the flame.

This couple worked on their relationship for some time, and they were able to recover their marriage. (By the way, the couple where the wife tore through my office? They also recovered.)

I've had others who didn't recover. There is no guarantee you're going to recover. But there are some things I'm going to tell you which can help the process, help tip the possibility in the direction of saving the relationship. What we're doing is trying to raise the chance that things are going to work out, that you're going to get back to your relationship. That's why I want to be very direct with you.

Let's first talk about what I consider to be the two primary types of affairs. Other experts describe subcategories which you might see elsewhere – "types" of affairs – for example, revenge affairs. To be sure, there are times when somebody did something wrong, whether it's infidelity or not and the other person decided to teach them a lesson by having an affair. That's a revenge affair. But even that example falls into a category I'm going to talk about; there was disconnection and there was no clear boundary.

From my vantage, those subcategories are rather unimportant at this point. They bring in distinctions for debate and discussion that do little to recover a relationship after an affair. These "types" of affairs may clarify some information when an affair is ongoing or developing, but they don't help much when you are working to recover.

Why Affairs Happen

So, let's keep it clear and simple. Disconnection and Lack of Boundaries.

First, I need to make a disclaimer of one other reason for affairs. If this reason applies to you, you need to go elsewhere and find some help, and then return to this material. I am referring to the affair that is based on addiction. It may be addiction to relationships; it may be addiction to sex. But it's completely about addiction.

Many people would rather sidestep the possibility that they suffer from addiction. But I have a slightly different view. We, as humans, are built for addiction. I say that even as I'm sitting beside my favorite addictive substance right now. I'm drinking a cup of coffee.

Right now, as I write this, it is in the afternoon. I'm drinking a cup of coffee. And that's my addiction, caffeine. Others might have an addiction to sugar or some other substance that's around them. Some find stronger, more mind/mood-altering substances – drugs or alcohol – as their source of addiction.

This "addictive nature" probably served us well millennia ago, when the source of addiction would not have been so plentiful. If you craved sweet things (for their instant energy source), it was no big deal. Fruit was only available for a short while each year. After that, you might have wanted something sweet, but it was not available.

Addiction is part of our DNA (which is not a reason to maintain an unhealthy addiction – just a reality for us all).

And some are addicted to sex.

The difference is that my coffee doesn't particularly interfere in my life. Every now and then, my kids roll their eyes when I run into Starbucks while we're at the mall, just to grab my coffee. But other than that, it really doesn't cause a lot of problems.

Let's talk about those who are addicted to relationships or sex. Really, in some ways, it breaks down by gender, but not entirely.

In gross generalities, it tends to be that women are addicted to relationships – that thrill, that rush of a relationship – and men tend toward addiction to sex (if that is their addiction).

There are women who are addicted to sex. But more often than not, it's men. Men usually are about the physical sex, not about the relationship. Again, I'm using gross generalities. So, let's just label this as "an affair fueled by addiction."

How do we know whether an affair is an addictive type or the other type (which is the "disconnected relationship type" – covered in-depth below)? It's very simple: There is a pattern to the addiction.

There is always a pattern to addiction. Some people may choose to ignore or avoid it, but there is a pattern: It doesn't matter how the marriage is going, there will be infidelity. If somebody is addicted, they'll go get their fix. After they get their fix, they go find another fix and they up the ante to get a bigger fix.

What you need to realize is it has nothing to do with that other person at all. It may seem to be, but it really isn't. It has to do with getting the fix, getting the hit, getting the "dopamine load" in the brain.

Here are some reasons why you might suspect addiction:

You have done things that are more and more thrilling and exciting in the act of sex. There are more chances of getting caught or pushing the boundaries of sexual encounters, just to make it more exciting.

You have to find something more exciting and someone more challenging, some area that's maybe more dangerous or risky. And if it involves, for instance, prostitutes, multiple participants, anonymous sex or things like that, then those are pretty clear signs that there is addiction.

Also, when there are multiple affairs, sex addiction is more likely to be a factor (or the factor). This is especially true if those multiple affairs tend to be short-term. Usually, the sex addict does not really want to try to manage and build a relationship. The addict is trying to get a "fix," not have a relationship.

If addiction to sex/relationships applies to you, the information in this book is of no use to you until you're in recovery. The starting point for any addiction is getting into recovery. If it applies, find some help, and then start restoring your relationship. Otherwise, what you are doing is dancing around the real issue, which is the addiction.

(There are many great resources, clinics, and therapists to help with the recovery process.)

Let me tell you why it's so important for you to start with recovery first and then address the relationship. In your efforts to recover after an affair, you need to regain the trust of your spouse. Let's say you regain your partner's trust and then start down this relationship recovery road. Then the addiction kicks in again, and you violate the boundaries of the relationship once more. Once again, your relationship is at risk – with even more barriers and a higher climb out.

Yes, you can recover from sexual addiction, and yes, you can save and recover a marriage after it. But the starting point for sexual or relational addiction is to get in recovery. If this applies to you, get started.

Now that we've bracketed off affairs of sexual addiction, let's talk about what I consider to be the main reason for affairs: disconnection in the relationship.

The lifeblood of marriage is connection. When that connection is missing, the relationship moves toward higher and higher risk for failure.

We are, as humans, built for that connection. We are "communal" creatures, needing contact with other humans. People don't generally do well in isolation because we are designed to have connection with others. More than that, humans crave and desire a closer connection with one other person. If it is not working in our primary relationship, we are going to look for it somewhere else. "Somewhere" generally means with other people.

Sometimes, we find that feeling of connection through our children, through friends, through work, through sports, through any number of other ways. We can usually find some people who make us feel like we have a level of connection. But there's still that deep yearning for a connection with that one person. It's that feeling of wanting to be embraced and merged with that one person. It is wired into us as humans. It's what often sends people looking for the other person or at least makes them vulnerable to that.

So, the main factor in affairs is the disconnection in the marriage. Another factor is the lack of boundaries. We don't have connection, and we don't have protection. At that point, the relationship is only waiting for the right circumstances for it to be in trouble.

What are the boundaries I'm talking about? Boundaries are how you protect your relationship, the safety factors that both protect and respect a chosen relationship. They mark the edges of your relationship. Think of it as a fence for the marriage, one that marks it for the spouses and for those on the "other side of the fence." For example, a person may decide, "I'm not going to speak to other people about my emotional life, I'll share that with my spouse." Or, "I'm not going to meet with someone of the opposite sex in a compromised situation, so I'm not going to meet them at a bar after work, or I'm not going to meet them for dinner. If I'm going to meet them for lunch in a place that is somewhat remote and somehow removed from business, I'm going to make sure there are others present."

Here are some other examples of boundaries: "I'm not going to communicate with an ex-girlfriend or ex-boyfriend on Facebook without the knowledge of my spouse." "I'm not going to e-mail. I'm not going to text these other people." "I'm not going to share my emotional life to any extent with anyone else."

I recognize these examples are broad statements. You may have a best friend with whom you share emotions. But here's the problem: I have heard so many justifications that I know you're better off over-protecting your marriage a bit than under-protecting it.

Marriages that are "affair proof" are well-connected and well-protected by boundaries.

If that's where you come from, if you say, "Okay, the reason this happened is (a) we were not connected, and (b) I did not protect the relationship," then you fall into the vast majority of affairs. These are the normal, everyday, run-of-the-mill affairs (if there is such a thing). This is the kind of affair that is addressable, which we can deal with.

Types of Connection

You may be wondering what to do now. You either recognize it is not addiction or have worked on the addiction. You realize that your marriage was not well-connected and the relationship was not protected. What do you do to move forward?

First, let's understand what happens in this connection. What we know from research is that the connection comes in two different variations: "adrenaline connection" and "endorphin connection."

My colleague, Bob Grant, offered the following explanation of the difference. Adrenaline connection is what happens in the beginning of any relationship. It's that magic of, "Oh, we just have so much in common, and I want to see this person," and it feels like you can't stay away from them. It's like a moth's attraction to light. That's a clear sign of adrenaline.

Now, this is where I want to shoot straight. You may justify that the affair really was about true love. But I'm going to tell you, it was about adrenaline.

A relationship, over time, must move to an endorphin connection. An endorphin connection is fueled when we do loving things towards the other person. It can include chemistry (the loving feelings); it's not that you suddenly are no longer attracted to this other person.

But the adrenaline fuel finally burns out. If we were to stay in that same infatuated period that starts every relationship, we would burn out our adrenal glands. It's true with a marriage; it's true with an affair.

If a relationship goes long enough, the adrenaline will burn through. And suddenly, we see the person for who they really are. That's the thing about affairs – while in the affair, you are not looking at the affair partner from a realistic perspective. You don't look at the person with whom you're having an affair with truthful eyes. You tend to exaggerate the good points, and you tend to play down the bad points. You tend to exaggerate the good times and forget the bad times. You live in a fantasy world when you're in an affair.

Then, you use that emotional charge of infatuation as a comparison. You pretend like it's real life and your married life is not. You forget that real life has kids and bills and jobs and other things.

Life is not always about finding a romantic little getaway, and a hotel room, and sneaking around, and going to nice dinners, and nice jewelry, and flowers, and all the other things that people get caught up in and then say, "Oh, that's true love."

No, that's adrenaline. No doubt about it, adrenaline is powerful. Our brain loves to get a hit of adrenaline because it leads to a hit of dopamine. There is nothing more powerful that motivates human behavior.

But, it just can't last.

The next step down in intensity is endorphins. The endorphins create a much slower burn on the dopamine load. The dopamine load from adrenaline has to be added onto – and added onto and added onto – and it's almost like you're kind of stoking the fire. And that's the problem: You can't keep stoking the fire. Adrenaline is laced with excitement and fear, leading to the dopamine cascade. Endorphins really are more tied to "feeling good for doing good." It is less tied to excitement and more tied to loving actions. You aren't getting a hit from doing exciting things, but by doing loving things.

(To be very clear, couples who are in long-term relationships can still do exciting things together. This isn't about settling for a "boring" life. It is just the difference between a connection fueled by adrenaline and a connection fueled by endorphins.)

Eventually, most affairs tend to fall apart for a couple of reasons. One is you finally get past that infatuation, and you realize the person wasn't all that you made them out to be. The second reason is you realize the person was willing to be dishonest with you (and you with them). This leads to the question of how you could ever fully trust each other in the future. When you hatch a relationship in dishonesty, at some point you must face the fact that dishonesty bites you back. You can't trust the other person moving forward. That's the nature of affairs.

Realistically, affair relationships don't tend to be the ones that make a lasting marriage. They tend to be soaked in dishonesty and deceit and, eventually, that's the death knell of it.

Often, part of what drives the intensity is that it's hidden and forbidden. You find yourself constantly thinking about this other person, but you can't talk about it to anyone. That drives up the intensity and fantasy of the relationship, further fueling the fire of adrenaline.

In other words, the affair is a potent, adrenaline-based attraction.

If you were really establishing a good, strong, healthy relationship, you'd be telling your friends about it. You would, from the very beginning, be telling them how wonderful he or she is.

But with an affair, you have to keep it quiet. When you keep it quiet, it's like putting it in a pressure cooker – the pressure builds, and builds, and builds – making it all seem more powerful than it really is. It's the hidden and forbidden that creates an "us versus the world" mentality.

You might have thought, "Everyone is going to be opposed to our relationship. They're not going to understand that it's true love." I've heard this many times.

Which brings us to the justifications that also emerge. Sometimes, people say, "Well, I wasn't getting my needs met in the relationship, so I looked elsewhere." That's justification. It assumes that your spouse was unwilling to meet those needs, and it also assumes these are needs that must be met (versus, for example, "wants"). Because if you're talking about sex, you may have to re-calculate that and say, "Wow, is that really something that I had to have, the way I wanted it, when I wanted it? Or was that just me caught up in my ego?" Because to be honest, that's where it comes from in affairs.

Also, some people tell me, "Well, it was purely physical." There is no such thing. While people often fool themselves, sex (and its physical connection) is never just physical. It creates a bonding between the people involved, fraught with emotional strings and attachments.

In a previous chapter, I discuss why sex is such a big issue in marriage and the fact that sex for humans is never just physical.

We know it from study after study. There is a connection formed between people who have sex that is unlike any other connection. It's not just physical. Think about the people you know who had sexual partners before they were married, perhaps in their younger years. They always have some kind of connection with that person. Why? Because it's woven into the act of sex as humans.

If you want to understand the nature of this, be sure to study chapter three. It will give you an idea of what happens with us physically during a sexual encounter. It's not just physical; that's just justification.

"It's true love," is the other justification (or rationalization). This is a difficult one for people to let go. They want to believe that they've found true love in the affair, because it gives the relationship meaning, that it isn't just an affair. If they return to the marriage (as I assume you have) they feel they've left this true love behind. This often leads to yearning and regret, which can undermine your efforts to recover.

The problem is people tend to compare the beginning of the affair relationship with the matured marriage relationship, instead of comparing the beginning of the affair with the beginning of the marriage – this compares them at unequal points. Many times, I ask people to compare the relationships at equal stages. They are often a bit surprised – and a bit deflated.

I've had this happen many times. People come to my office and say, "I found the man/woman of my dreams, and my spouse is nothing like them." I say, "Well, tell me about this person." After they tell me about this new person, I say, "Okay, now tell me about your spouse when you first got together," and they do. I often have to point out, "You're experiencing the same feelings. Except now you're comparing an issue-laden relationship filled with unresolved pains and hurts with one that's fresh and doesn't have any pains and hurts to be dealt with yet."

There is one other complication to this scenario. Humans have a propensity to re-cast memories to match what we now feel and believe. Memories are not factual snap-shots, but changeable thoughts, which we rebuild to match what is currently happening, allowing us to remain consistent in our self-view.

In other words, many people will re-remember the early stages of the marital relationship and say there were no strong emotions of infatuation and attraction. Yet, spousal, family, and friend memories contradict this, as do letters and cards. And if they exist, personal journals often contradict those memories as well.

It can be painful to admit that there is a consistent path of relating at the beginning of all relationships. And it probably applies to both the marriage and the affair.

Allow me to be very direct: True love is not based on dishonesty and deceit. That is an antecedent to having any kind of real love. If you're involved in a relationship and having an affair, it's not true love. It's infatuation; it's fueled by adrenaline and built on deceit. So really, how could it be true love? Deceit is not a path toward love.

People also will say, "I never felt this way before," to which I say, "Our brain tricks us very often." You may not remember feeling this way. But guess what? You won't remember feeling this way next time, either. Because the only time where you are aware of this state in the brain is when you're in it, at that moment. Our brain is so full of chemicals in that infatuation period that it completely clouds out a realistic memory of how we used to feel at other times.

Think about the phrase, "madly in love." What we know from brain studies is that it's literal. A person in the infatuation period shows very similar brain function as someone who is mentally ill. The brain is so overcooked on adrenaline and dopamine, the neurons say, "I've never felt this way before." You are fooled into thinking this way, and you have a hard time remembering how other connections felt. These justifications tend to get people stuck in the affair.

In many ways, this makes the affair a very addictive process.

So, what is the difference between the addiction affair and the disconnected affair? In an addiction affair, the motivation was, from the beginning, to get the fix. The person is addicted to getting sex or having a relationship. The other person is fairly irrelevant to that (although self-justification sometimes covers this fact).

In a disconnected-fueled affair, it is an attempt to find connection. But it leads to a strong (even addictive) connection with someone else.

Instead of recovering from an addiction, you are breaking an intense (and therefore addictive) connection with a particular person.

As you have probably experienced, it is hard to get away from that intense connection, that addictive feel. How do you break that addictive feel? You need to get away from the fuel of the addiction. This is the tough part because you don't want to. You don't want to break it off because it feels like you're giving up something powerful, something real.

Every time I hear this, my advice is always the same: "You've got to break off the relationship completely." And they struggle and struggle with it until they finally break off communication (assuming they really want to save the marriage). It takes awhile, but somewhere around the three- to six-week mark, they come in and say, "I don't know what I was thinking. This person is possessive and angry and vindictive, and they're not attractive . . ." The list of negative descriptors goes on and on, but they can't see it while the adrenaline clouds their eyes.

They can't see it while the dopamine fix is making the "love." Really, infatuation is blind; love is wide-eyed, wide open, looking at who the person really is and saying, "That's the person I love." Infatuation is choosing to see everything is good by ignoring evidence to the contrary.

(Let me be clear here that I do not believe a marital partner is completely perfect and an affair partner is completely imperfect. In fact, love is really about seeing people for who they really are, and accepting them that way. In an affair, though, it is often skewed to see the affair partner as far more perfect and the spouse as far more imperfect than an objective view would show.)

At this point, you may not particularly like what I am saying. So let me assure you that my intention is to help you save your marriage and see the affair from a realistic perspective.

You may be asking, "What do I do? I've had an affair, but my spouse doesn't know yet." I'm going to tackle this first because it's the beginning point when a spouse does not know: "Do I tell or do I not tell?"

This question has actually been researched. Studies have shown that whether you tell or not, the outcome can be the same. Your efforts will either cause the marriage to fall apart or come together. Telling your spouse about the affair is not a guarantee it's going to work out; not telling is not a guarantee it's going to work out, either.

Either choice can work for or against you. So, I have a question for you to ask yourself: What are your reasons for telling or not telling?

That question gives us insight into your motivation.

Some people will say to me, "I can't tell my spouse because my spouse has already said, 'If you have an affair, I'll leave you.'" In this situation, the person says, "I am 100% convinced that my spouse is telling me the truth, that an affair is a marriage-ender. So if I want to save my marriage, I cannot tell." That's one category. And it may lead to not telling. (Although I have seen many marriages recover, even though a spouse had at one point proclaimed an affair would be a marriage-ender – theory and practice are two different things.)

Then, there are those who say, "My spouse and I treasure being honest and open and even though it may hurt, I think we can work through this." That would be a reason to tell.

Sometimes, I even have people tell me, "I don't want to carry this around in my gut, in my heart," to which I would say that's not a reason to tell or not to tell.

If you're feeling overwhelmed with guilt and think the way of relieving it is to tell, understand that's not the reason to do it. If you have done something wrong, then you have to decide whether it's going to be helpful to tell or not to tell. Don't do it because you want to "get it off your chest." That only shifts it to the other person. You may be saying, "Whew, I feel better," but the spouse is now devastated.

The question to consider is: Whose need is being met by telling? If it's a relational need – that you have to be honest and open and that's how you'll get through this – then that's a reason to tell. If it's your need to get it off your chest because you don't want to have to carry it around, then you're just handing the load of crap over to your spouse to carry around; there will be incredible pain associated with this type of telling.

Whether you tell or you don't tell, you first need to ask yourself three things. "Why am I going to tell?" "Whose need am I trying to deal with?" And finally, "What is the desired outcome I want from this?" When you make a decision on telling or not telling, the decision is final. Let me be clear about that. If you say, "I can't tell," then you have chosen to take that to your grave with you.

If you say, "I will tell," you have to take that decision through the rest of your life also. Either way, it goes with you forward.

Over the years, I've worked with people who had an affair, decided not to tell, and recovered the relationship. Years later, the secret is eating at them, and they finally decide they just have to come clean. They confess, and the marriage (which had been saved and restored) ends. Why? Because suddenly, everything has been a lie in the eyes of the spouse. If you decide not to tell, realize that it's a lifetime decision. You may then choose to live your life with that piece as the motivator to step up into a different place in your life, to a higher place. In other words, you have learned from your mistake and will use it as fuel for self-improvement.

You can decide to live a life of full integrity, and you can decide to relate in a way that builds your marriage to the point that it is safe, and you can commit to making sure that you never put the relationship at risk again.

Which brings us to step one of your process: raising your personal standards.

Somewhere along the way, you likely broke your own standard of what you expected of yourself. I don't know many people who say, "You know what? I set out to have an affair. I planned to go do it. I headed out to the bar (or wherever), I met this person for lunch and dinner and dates. I did it because I knew I would find somebody."

There are such people out there, but they are not likely reading this book since they are not really working on their relationship. That's a whole different category of people. Such people often fit into the earlier category I talked about and suffer from addiction.

If you sought out an affair, rather than finding yourself falling into an affair, that's a clear symptom of addiction.

But if you found yourself caught up in a situation that got out of control, then you need to ask, "What are the standards I need to set for myself? How am I going to be protective of the relationship? How am I going to be protective of my own boundaries and the boundaries of the marriage?" You can raise your standards for yourself.

To be clear, I am not singling you out as being different. We all have places to grow, standards to raise, boundaries to protect. I'm constantly asking myself, "Okay, what's my next standard to meet? How can I go after a higher goal in life?" Whether it's my physical, mental, spiritual, or psychological life, I'm looking for the next standard I need to step up to. I'm inviting you to use this as a time to ask, "Okay, what's the next standard for me to meet?" Because you need to raise the standard to make sure that you insulate yourself and your marriage from an affair ever happening again.

Then, you want to begin to set the boundaries of the relationship.

What do you need to do to make sure you don't get into that place again? These are the boundaries, the ways you make sure you protect the marriage. This is not about what you need to do with the connection in the relationship. This is the protection part. What do you need to actively do/stop doing to protect the marriage? For example, some people say, "I'm going to stop business travel because that puts me at risk." "I'm going to stop hanging out at the bar because that puts me at risk." "I'm going to stop going dancing because that puts me at risk." "I'm going to stop interacting on Facebook with this person because it puts me at risk." Boundaries are about looking at the things that put you at risk for breaking the bounds of the marriage. These are specific areas or actions where you say, "I'm going to stop that; I'm going to protect the relationship."

This is a golden opportunity for you and your spouse, as a couple, to say, "What clear boundaries do we draw around our relationship? What do we need to do to protect it?" This is not "What do we need to do to reconnect?" This is about protection.

The connection is going to take some effort. With a spouse who has been hurt – where the trust has been ruptured – understand that it's going to take some time and effort to rebuild. You first start with, "Where are the places I need to create protection?" The protection needs to be there, so that the connection has a chance to develop. But they are separate issues.

When you married, if you had the same vows that I did, you made a promise to forsake all others. What you likely didn't promise is to always feel gushy and connected. The first thing to decide is, "How do we do that? How do we forsake all others? How do we make sure that we protect that part of our life?"

To be clear, the connection is important in helping to protect your marriage. But the boundaries are necessary when the connection wanes. It sets the safety zone in which the connection can grow.

To me, the North Star of any relationship is commitment. If you live in the Northern Hemisphere, the North Star is always present at night, pointing toward north. It gives the point of reference for navigating, no matter where you might be. Lost? Locate the North Star and navigate from there.

In a marriage, that point is "commitment." If you use that as your navigation point, you can rely on the commitment to take you through when you're not feeling all the warm feelings you once felt.

I've heard it said that commitment is doing what you agreed to do when you no longer feel the way you did when you made that agreement. That's commitment. What do you need to do to protect your commitment? Be specific in your mind. How do you need to interact with other people? Where do you not need to be? Where do you need to be? What do you need to do to maintain accountability? What can you do to make sure those attitudes, decisions, and actions are in place? That's step one.

Step two is becoming transparent with your spouse. After the trust is ruptured, you realize one very central thing: trust is a gift. It's always a gift. The reason I say that is because some people will make trust very, very costly. They won't trust anyone. Other people make trust way too cheap. They repeatedly trust people who repeatedly break their trust. Those are the two ends of the spectrum: one never lets anybody in, and one always lets everybody in.

When somebody has an affair, it ruptures the trust of the relationship. At some point in the recovery process, a spouse is going to have to say, "Okay, I'm going to trust you again. I'm going to decide to trust you again." In other words, "I'm going to begin to give you the gift of trust, but your role is to treasure it."

You can't earn somebody's trust; you can only protect it or destroy it. You can't earn it because it has to be given. You can be trustworthy; part of that is being transparent – becoming transparent about where you are, what you're doing, who you're with and what's happening there.

Unfortunately, because of the affair, you're going to have to put up with your spouse feeling the need to play detective and checking up on you. In the chapter where I spoke about what to do if your spouse had an affair, I suggested being very careful about the questions they ask and encouraged them to not play detective.

I'm giving you, the person who had the affair, the opposite advice. Be transparent and be willing to let the other person see everything. If they text you and say, "Hey, where are you?" tell them. And if they say, "What are you doing?" tell them. If they need reassurance, recognize that's the cost of your actions. That's what it's going to take to rebuild this.

Being transparent may mean that you have to hand over your phone whenever it's asked for without there being a whole lot of deleted texts and numbers. In other words, be sure there is nothing to hide.

You might need to give up your e-mail password. I've already suggested to your spouse to not be going in and always looking at your phone and e-mails. If you want to rebuild trust, though, your spouse may need to do that. You've got to give your spouse the opportunity to do that.

If your spouse says, "I want to see your Facebook messaging," you show it immediately. You do not say, "Well, let me give you my computer in a day (or in an hour)," or "Let me turn it on (or log-in) first." Let your spouse do it. Find ways to be 100% transparent, knowing that it won't be forever. Do it long enough for your spouse to say, "Okay, I see that you have changed."

And remember, you need to have changed. You need to have raised your standard to become somebody different so your spouse can say, "Okay now I trust you, I see the difference." Because your spouse needs to see the change. There are only a couple of options, and the only one that matters is you realizing that you have to be different in the world, that you have a higher standard, that you have clearer boundaries, that you have to protect the relationship. Until that happens, your spouse is going to be stuck feeling like there's always that chance of something being hidden, of something happening again.

In the beginning, I said affairs are caused by the fact that boundaries were not clear and there was not enough connection, and you didn't have your standard set high enough to avoid it. But, now you've raised your standards and created boundaries, right?

Now, you have to create the connection. It's going to take some effort because the spouse who has been hurt is going to be less desirous of being connected, so you have to work on that slowly. (We will talk about building connection together in another chapter.)

The last thing I suggest you do is find a way to create accountability for yourself. Find a friend who will hold you accountable so your spouse doesn't have to always do it.

That's a tough role for both of you; when your spouse holds you accountable, at some point you may end up resenting your spouse who's only trying to protect the relationship. But it can feel as if they're playing sheriff and judge. This is where it gets tough. You broke the trust of the relationship, and you may struggle with your spouse who wants to protect it.

So, find some outside accountability. There are men's accountability groups all over the place, and there are women's groups as well. A good friend, a best friend, to whom you can say, "Hey, I need you to know this happened and I need you to be asking me, 'Are you holding up your end of the bargain?'" Accountability is crucial for making sure that you know somebody's going to hold you responsible and it doesn't have to just be your spouse.

Okay, that's a lot of tough stuff coming at you. I hope you understand I've been shooting pretty straight with you. Here's the reason: I think that marriages can come out on the other side of an affair stronger than they went in. I think many marriages can make it through an affair and actually use it as an impetus for being a much stronger relationship than it was before – if you use it as an opportunity for growth and change. If you don't, if you try to sidestep it, if you try to play it down, if you try to justify it, it will become a cancer and eat away at the relationship.

If you face it head on and make yourself trustworthy, if you raise your own personal standards, if you create the boundaries that are necessary in a relationship, and if you create accountability, you will be at a new point where you can say, "Okay, I need to move beyond this."

You have to forgive yourself and seek the forgiveness of your spouse, but you can make it a stronger relationship. I didn't say you will, I said you can. This is your opportunity. Don't let a mistake weigh you down; don't let a mistake mark your life.

Instead, rise above it. See this as a place where you can create a relationship that is affair-proof and that you will treasure for the rest of your life.

Chapter 6

FORGIVING AFTER INFIDELITY

Forgiving is a part of life – a central part of life. I believe that the forgiveness process is what allows us to keep moving forward in a healthy way and also what connects us with others. This is true not only with life-in-general but with life-after-infidelity.

Not everyone likes to hear me say that!

When I say that to people, especially those struggling with a spouse's infidelity, occasionally they get angry with me. Some have said, "How dare you tell me to forgive them! I can't just let them off the hook like that." A few people say, "Well, I would love to forgive, but they haven't asked for forgiveness." And I have had others tell me they had nothing they needed to forgive; what the person had done was unforgivable, and therefore they were not going to forgive. They would rather hold onto their anger, remind themselves of what had happened, and armor themselves with it. Those are all recipes for staying stuck.

Let me tell you about "Bob." Bob told me that he didn't know how he could possibly forgive his wife for having an affair. He didn't know how he could possibly forgive her for betraying their marriage, all the while portraying herself as the model wife. I understand those feelings, but they completely miss the point of forgiving. You see, there is a piece of us that tends to get stuck in the "forgiveness trap." And so I wanted to spend a little bit more time teasing that apart in this chapter.

Let's look at what forgiveness is about and how you get there. There are six different steps to go through in order to get to forgiveness, but you first need to decide you want to forgive. Which brings us face-to-face with the problem of misunderstanding in very fundamental ways this whole forgiveness process.

When I was a child, my older brother and I got into our fair share of spats. I remember more than once, having our father's fairly strong and very eager hands on each of our shoulders, kind of by the scruffs of our necks, holding us face to face, and making us apologize to each other. One of us would have to say, "I'm sorry." And then the other one would say, "I forgive you. I'm sorry, too" and the first would respond, "I forgive you, too."

But we didn't feel it. We forgave under duress because we "had to." And what we learned from that is something that we all have tended to learn in our culture: forgiveness is somehow related to the other person. Because of that, one way we can control what happens in our lives is to choose when we're going to forgive and not forgive. We somehow believe we are holding the other person hostage with our choice to forgive or not.

This is the place where I think we've done a tremendous disservice to our children, to ourselves, to everyone in our culture; we make forgiveness something that is for the other person. The heart of forgiving is letting go of the pain. Not letting the other person off the hook, but letting go of the pain. That doesn't mean it's an instant fix. It's not like you say, "I forgive you," and you're all good. The pain stays for a bit. But healing can come into the space that's created when you commit to forgiving.

Before we go further into this process of forgiving, let me remind you that anger is a secondary emotion. The primary emotion is hurt/threat. Anger is often what captures us and others around us. But it is always secondary to the hurt/threat. We may tell ourselves that forgiving is letting go of the anger, but it is really about releasing the hurt.

Here's what generally happens when we don't find a path to forgiveness: First, something happens that hurts us. That hurt is kind of like the initial injury, and then the anger comes out of that hurt. Anger is what happens when the hurt is unresolved. And if the anger is unresolved, it leads to resentment – which is simply anger that has gotten stuck in the system. I like to think of it kind of like an accident. Something happens, something hits you, and it injures you. It hurts. The anger is kind of like the big red welt that shows on the outside. It doesn't show the pain you feel, but it shows this mark where the injury happened. That's the anger.

Then, if that injury does not heal, the resentment is kind of like an infection from that injury. Anger is the initial bodily response of inflammation, and redness, and maybe some bleeding. And then the resentment is more like that infection that gets in and starts to spread. When it spreads, it begins to be much more dangerous.

Resentment left to fester long enough leads to disdain, and that's when we make the other person the enemy. It's not just that we're angry with them, or that we're seething underneath with anger, but we begin to see them as being fundamentally flawed. We see them as malicious people, nasty people. They are the evil person on the other side, and we're the victim. That's when we begin to find ourselves in trouble.

When you don't forgive, you keep yourself as the victim in the story. We'll get to that more in-depth later in this chapter.

There is another option, and that's to say, "What's my responsibility?" (By that I mean, "What is my 'ability to respond'?") When I use the word "responsibility," some believe I mean "blame." Some people have said, "Oh, so this is my fault?"

Responsibility has nothing to do with blame or fault. It has to do with realizing that you have a role to play in any interaction. We get stuck in victim mode when we say, "I'm not going to forgive." The irony is that when we refuse to forgive, we think we are holding the other person responsible, when in reality what we're really doing is isolating ourselves by playing the role of a victim.

Another life precept I teach is that each person needs to be 100% responsible for their lives. Some think that's unfair. Others think it's a tall order. But that is really a misunderstanding about being responsible.

When I say you need to be 100% responsible in your life, I'm saying that you have 100% control of your responses. You're "able to respond." That's "response-ability." When we confuse that with blame, then we're stuck in another place.

When we blame others, we keep ourselves stuck as the victim of our own story. Understand the other person is usually unaware and/or unaffected by this. They're going on with their life, completely sidestepping whatever blame is being thrown at them. They are disconnected from the fact you are holding onto the pain.

Sometimes, it isn't blaming the other person. Instead, we blame ourselves. That is just another way to avoid 100% responsibility. When we blame ourselves, it keeps us stuck as "less than," as undeserving, as once again a victim. "You shouldn't have done that to me," makes me a victim. "I shouldn't have left myself open for that," keeps me stuck in that victim role. Unless I then ask, "What am I going to do next? How am I going to respond to this situation?"

One way to respond is by choosing to forgive, by choosing to let go of the hurt, the pain, the anger, the resentment.

The forgiveness process is about moving from enemy to empathy. The danger of refusing to forgive is that you make the other person the enemy in ways that also make it impossible to move forward. Not just in the relationship, but in any other way.

So, why don't we all choose to forgive? There are some misunderstandings we carry around about forgiveness that may render us unwilling to forgive. These misunderstandings are where people often get stuck. You may say, "So you're telling me to forgive and forget." Absolutely not. I'm not saying to forget, first because that is virtually impossible. Lacking a good case of amnesia, you're going to remember.

Forgiveness is really more about understanding it in a different way. I'm not talking about remembering it as if it didn't happen – that's denial – nor am I talking about remembering the details differently than they happened. You need to understand that there are some other dynamics in place. These dynamics are alive in the other person, and they are alive within you. These dynamics are the ways you both are viewing the world, yourselves, and the events as they unfold. We are not just victims of the situation; instead, we are part of the process. The other person is not the enemy, not evil, but is fully human, just like we are.

When you refuse to forgive, in some ways, you give an inordinate amount of strength and power to that other person. You are saying they have the capacity of wounding you so badly it leaves you forever stuck to that story. Whether you want to reconcile with someone, or whether you want to always stay away from them, you still need to forgive. This is about moving forward and seeing that person as someone who doesn't have such power over you.

I recently had someone in my office who kept telling me how she was holding onto just such a situation in her life. I pointed out that she continues to allow that person to live within her life, to remain an active part, even though she'd cut this person off and there had been no actual contact in 20 years. Refusing to forgive kept her captive to the story and the person for all that time.

Forgiveness lets you get the person out of your life if necessary, or allows for restoration of the relationship if possible.

The Forgiveness Process

There is a step-by-step path to forgiveness; it's not complex. In fact, the process is quite simple. But, that doesn't make it easy. As you go through the process, you will notice there are places where you will protest. That is a typical response. It tells you that you are bumping up against one of your barriers to forgiveness. If a step seems too easy, you may have already managed that step – or you may find that you thought it was easy, but your feelings may not be so quick to follow. Be patient with yourself. True forgiveness takes some time and perhaps some tears. The only path to forgiveness is through it. So, let's get started.

Step One

How do you move from seeing the other person as an enemy, to having empathy? That really is one of the major shifts that have to happen in order to forgive. You have to be able to move from enemy to empathy. How do you do that?

One way is to acknowledge the other person is not your true enemy. We often create scenarios where we have the good and bad forces in our lives, and we see "evilness" in other people. What we fail to see is that people generally are acting to help themselves, not primarily to hurt other people. Notice that distinction. People are primarily acting for themselves – to somehow preserve their self-image, or their standing in society, or whatever else may be going on. They're trying to preserve a part of themselves. Inadvertently, that may cause hurt for another person.

Allow me, just for a moment, to tread on some pretty thin ice. Let's say there has been infidelity in a relationship. It's very easy to talk about the offending spouse as being corrupt and horrible, as mistreating the relationship and unfair to the vows, making them into an evil person. Or you can say, "What was going on with them? What was there within them that they were trying to find some place of connection with another person, or trying to deal with an addictive thought process in their life?"

What if they were not evil, but they were ordinary people who have ordinary human foibles, shortcomings, and failings? What if, instead of seeing them as being an evil person (which it's easy to turn them into), you start seeing them as somebody who made a horrible error, likely because something was going on within them? It would be much easier to paint a story of good and evil, but it would also not be as nuanced as our lives really are.

There is this thought process scientists have noticed called the Attribution Error. It has been noted within philosophy and religion for millennia. The Attribution Error says, "If you do something wrong, there is a character flaw within you; but if I do something wrong, it's simply a mistake." We might both do the exact same thing wrong, but when I look at you, I claim you did it because something is wrong with you. Yet when I look in the mirror, I believe I made a simple mistake, which is easy to understand in the context of my life. In other words, we let ourselves off the hook and hold other people accountable.

One of the often-quoted verses from the Bible tells us before we look at the speck in our neighbor's eye, we better look at the plank in our own eye. That's the Attribution Error. It's easy to hold someone accountable for something they've done in their life that we would excuse or ignore in our own life.

When we want to start the process of forgiveness, step one is to see the other person as a human, foibles and all, likely to make this mistake, and many other mistakes (just like us). Sometimes, when others do something wrong, we see them as being a horrible person ("the slime of the earth," as more than one client has noted). In reality, they're human, making human errors, doing things that we wish they hadn't done; but they probably did them mostly for their own good. They are not out to get us. That begins to shift the equation away from taking it so personally.

Step Two

Step two is just a decision. It's making a decision to forgive. When you decide to forgive, you reclaim your personal power. If you say, "I cannot forgive," you've given up control of your life and your capacities. You've given up control, all the while pretending that you are in control. If you say you cannot forgive, you may as well be saying, "I'm holding this as a self-righteous place," but in reality, all you've done is give up control to that event, and that person. A decision to forgive is saying, "I'm going to take back my own power."

Step two is deciding to forgive. Notice, there's a difference between that decision, and when it finally happens. Forgiveness is a process. It's not a moment in time; it takes some time and some processing, but it begins with a decision.

Once you make the decision you're going to forgive, it doesn't instantly take away all of the pain. It also doesn't instantly take away all of the hurts and frustrations. It simply begins a process of healing in your life. Many people falter on this seemingly easy step. They just can't quite get that sentence out: "I choose to forgive." Remember, you don't necessarily need to say that to the other person. But you do need to clearly say it to yourself.

By clearly stating, "I choose to forgive," you reassert your personal power. You acknowledge it is a choice. You also draw a line in the sand between Unforgiveness and Forgiveness. That is a powerful decision.

Which leads us to step three.

Step Three

When those memories resurface – and they will when you think of that person or that event – breathe through the memories and thoughts.

When I say "breathe through," I am referring to belly breathing. If you're not familiar with belly breathing, it's the same technique taught in meditation, yoga, martial arts, musical training, and other disciplines. Belly breathing is a method used to calm yourself down.

If you have never done it before, simply lie down on the floor, the couch, or your bed. Put one hand over your belly button and the other over your breastbone. Concentrate on your breathing until the only hand that moves with your breathing is the one over your belly button. It's easiest when you're lying down because you can see which hand is moving. But once you've figured out how to do it while lying down, you can do it while you're walking, sitting, standing, driving, or any other time.

Whenever the memories hit you, just belly breathe. Deep, slow breaths. In and out. Many people find the "Box Breathing" method works well for belly breathing. Imagine a box with a three-count on each side. Starting at the base of the box, you breathe in for a count of three as you move up to the top of the box, then hold the breath for a count of three across the top of the box. As you move down the other side of the box, you exhale for a count of three, then hold the exhale for a count of three (some find it more comfortable to hold the exhale for a count of two). Imagine that box with each calming breath.

Why belly breathe through those thoughts? When you experience painful memories, it triggers the threat portion of your brain, which triggers your body to go on alert. When that happens, you end up reinforcing the feeling of threat, hurt, and anger. And that threat part of the brain? It is so old it doesn't even understand language. So you can't just tell yourself, "It's alright. There's no problem." It assumes those memories and thoughts are happening right now, creating that physical response. And really, it is the bodily sensation that is so upsetting and disturbing to us. But breathing goes beyond the non-verbal nature. It lets your brain know that everything's okay. (I have further details on why this is true <in training HERE>.)

Those memories are going to be there. You're going to feel the pain for a moment. But what we're trying to do with this process is let the grief and hurt pass. The body and mind are designed to release the pain unless we allow it to get stuck and hold onto it. So, it is important to learn to let the pain pass through the body. This is not the same as trying to stay away from it; it is choosing to not hold onto it.

Often, what we tend to do when we have those thoughts is to hold onto them, nurture them, give them more energy – we "entertain" the thoughts.

I love the mental image of entertaining a thought. It's kind of like we're taking it out and we're doing a little juggling with it, playing with it, turning it around and looking at it. We're interacting with it. All that does is keep our body in an alert, and angry, and frustrated place. If, instead, we have a memory and remind ourselves to breathe through it, we're letting that memory pass, which is what it needs to do. Let it pass, and move forward. There's no need to sit there and try to process through a thought. Notice how often we humans like to try to figure things out. ("What was that all about?" "Why did they do that?" "What were they meaning?") Instead, we should just say, "You know what? I don't know what they were thinking, but I'm not going to get wrapped up in it."

Having a thought and holding a thought are two very different things. Thoughts arrive on their own (that's just what our minds do). We get to choose how long we allow them to stay.

When I spent all day (every day) in my office talking with people, one of my basic rules was that we were not going to talk much about "why." ("Why did this happen?" "Why did that person do this?" "Why is this going on?") Because doing so was useless. It was just a way of playing with our thoughts. In reality, it is acting as if we could gain some control if we could just find the motivation behind it, instead of acknowledging that sometimes things happen, and people do things, and we don't benefit from teasing them apart.

You don't have to process or pick apart someone else's thoughts, because you can't. You won't get it right because you don't know what's going on in their mind. You won't make any progress. You'll stay stuck in your pain for as long as you decide that you're going to entertain that thought process. As long as you decide you're going to hang onto it, it will stay. You need to breathe through it. Instead of resisting it or forcing it, just let it pass. Acknowledge the pain that it causes you and let it pass through your body. Acknowledge that it can even feel physically painful, but as you breathe through it, feel it dissipating from your body. When you do, it will process properly like it's supposed to, instead of being stuck like it's not supposed to.

We're not designed to hold onto those thoughts/hurts, even when we're at our best. Yet, when we're at our worst, when we are working from that place of threat and hurt, we tend to hold onto them. We don't need to; we need to react from a higher place of forgiveness and acceptance and keep processing them – it is, I believe, what we're naturally designed to do. So, step three is to breathe through the memories and let them pass. Don't try to force them out, but don't try to interact with them. Just let them pass.

Step Four

Step four is accepting the lessons from the incident while allowing the hurt to evaporate. There are always lessons we can learn from tough and painful events; it's how we're designed to grow and mature. Lessons are always found in adversity. How much we grow is based on how we handle adversity.

I want you to think back for a minute to the times and places where you learned the most about yourself – about who you are and how you want your life to be. Chances are, the lessons came as a result of adversity. Looking back, many people can see how their biggest barriers and struggles led to life changes and moments of growth. Adversity teaches us deep lessons in ways that normal times just can't.

But there is a choice. When adversity comes, we will either learn and grow or fall into victim mode. Part of the lesson is to learn how to grow. When we only see ourselves as a victim, we don't truly learn any useful lessons. We learn a lesson of "lack" and of danger, but not of growth and possibility. When we face adversity and painful events, we need to say, "How do I grow from this in positive ways? What do I learn from this? How do I learn to be more empathetic? How do I learn more about myself? How do I learn more about other people around me?" Then and only then can we capitalize on that adversity and learn a lesson from it. Those are tough lessons, but usually the strongest ones of life.

Remember, sometimes forgiveness teaches us that there are people we need to stay away from. It shows us people who are dangerous to us. And that's a good lesson as long as we don't apply it to everyone. "That person is a danger" is a different lesson than "People are a danger."

Perhaps, through this forgiveness process, you will realize that you CAN forgive, but you CAN'T reunite. That can be tough, but it's also important. You may realize that the infidelity is not a singular event. It may represent a pattern of disregard. If so, the outcome MAY be that you can't be a part of such a relationship. Just be clear on the reasons for this. Be sure it is not because of anger/hurt, nor because you refuse to forgive.

Step Five

Step five is where it can get a bit painful – and personal. Step five is to accept your role, using that as another point (or potential) for change and growth. What role did you play in being in an unfaithful relationship (again, not for the actions of infidelity, but being in that relationship)? Perhaps it was ignoring the signs about the relationship, or not responding in ways that would have set up clear and appropriate boundaries. Perhaps it was your part of the disconnect between the two of you. What role did you play?

Here is the tough realization: We all play a role in the story of our own lives, even when things happen to us which we have no control over, and which are not our fault. We still have a role; this is not about fault, not about "How did I cause this to happen?" What role did you play?

For instance, let's return to infidelity. Remember that infidelity, with the exception of addictive reasons, comes out of a disconnected relationship (and lacking clear, strong boundaries).

The person who committed the affair is completely 100% responsible for the actions of the infidelity. But both people are responsible for having been in a disconnected relationship. It takes two people to stay in a disconnected relationship. When somebody has cheated, the person who was cheated upon has to say, "What role did I play in the backdrop of that?" Not in a "spouse being unfaithful" role (because there's always another alternative to committing adultery), but "What role did I play in being part of a disconnected relationship?"

I know this is a hard one to grasp, and that it's particularly tough if you feel so wronged that you want to hold onto it. I'm asking you to step back and say, "What was my role in that disconnection process? Where was I?"

I was talking with an acquaintance one day. He was telling me this long story about a painful breakup with his girlfriend. The story went on and on about this painful breakup – it was like listening to a country-western song. The girlfriend had "done him wrong," and done him dirty, and cheated on him, and he could not believe it. When I finally said, "So, tell me what your role was in this." He resisted and resisted. I said, "No, go back and tell me the whole story again, but this time, tell me all the places where you had a role in it."

Sure enough, there was one place where he had a big role: They had already been having problems, but he had buried his head in the sand about it. He looked back and said, "Oh, it wasn't about the cheating, but wow – I should have seen the signs here, and I could have taken action there, and I let it slide there."

Suddenly, he was aware of where he fit in a dysfunctional relationship that he had blamed totally on her, with him playing the role of victim over and over. He remained the victim in the whole scenario until he began to acknowledge he had a role in the process.

It wasn't his fault she cheated on him; he realized he had been in a relationship with someone who was not going to treat him well. Instead of facing the situation and acting, he ignored it.

He allowed the process to go downhill, rather than taking action to fix it (either by working on it or leaving). That's learning the lesson and accepting your role.

Until you have accepted your role in the process, it is hard to release it. You are always a victim of the circumstances.

BIG NOTE FOR CLARITY: There ARE times when people are victims in life. They may be caught in an unforeseen weather event. War may break out. They may be in the same room as a terrorist about to take action. They may find themselves in the path of a runaway vehicle on a peaceful street. But for most inter-relational problems, we have a role to play. I am not saying every bad event in a person's life is their fault. It isn't about karma, or "attraction," or any other philosophy. This is about seeing that relationships are dances, with steps being danced by all participants.

Step Six

Step six is to reinforce your choice to forgive. You have to keep reminding yourself, "I want to forgive, and I choose to forgive," because our primitive brain doesn't want us to forgive. That primitive brain, way deep in the human skull, is built to look for threats. One reason for holding onto hurts is to remind us of what seems like a threat. "Better safe than sorry," is the motto of that primitive brain.

That primitive brain keeps telling us, "Don't forget this! Remember this person, and what they did. Stay away from them!" It wants us to grab hold of it, delve into it, and hold tightly to it. So, step six is to reinforce your choice to forgive. This is where we begin to ask, "Do I need to have boundaries? Do we need to either avoid this other person or create some other clear boundaries? How are we going to deal with this other person?"

Why is this a step in forgiveness? Because it is difficult to stay at a place of unforgiveness if you allow yourself to once again risk being hurt in the same way. Taking action to shore up your boundaries and the boundaries of the relationship allows you to release the hurt and move toward forgiveness.

Here's the thing: forgiveness and justice are not related. Forgiveness and reconciliation are separate events. There is a separation between the process of forgiveness and whether there is justice, or whether there is reconciliation. Not forgiving keeps you stuck, yet does nothing to the other person. That's why we want to forgive. It does nothing to the other person to not forgive.

Justice occurs externally to the process of forgiving. If something happens to the other person because of what they did, it's external to the process of you letting go of the pain. These are two different processes. Holding a grudge imprisons you, not the other person.

Let me be clear: forgiveness and reconciliation are two different processes. I can forgive someone and still decide to not be in a relationship with them. If I want to be in a relationship with someone, I have to forgive them; otherwise, there cannot be reconciliation. But, just because I forgive, it doesn't mean I have to also reconcile.

Think of the powerful example of Pope John Paul II when he was shot. Afterward, he offered forgiveness to the person who shot him. He visited the assailant in his prison cell and forgave that person. Then he left the prison – and he also left the prisoner in his cell. There was still a penalty to what happened, and that's an important distinction. Forgiveness is an internal process. Reconciliation and justice are external processes that are separate from the forgiving process.

Which leads me to the place of asking you: if you find something you will not forgive, why? What are you holding onto? What are you getting out of it? What's your fear of forgiving?

Because when we get right down to it, many people get to the place where they're ready to forgive and then something scares them about the process. What is your fear about forgiving? Here's a tough question: What will you give up if you forgive?

What we often have to give up is the belief we had no role in the process – when in fact, we did. We have to give up that place where we are the victim, where the other person is entirely at fault. What is it that you will have to give up if you forgive? What is threatened in your self-understanding, or your understanding of the other person, if you forgive? What's at risk?

Ask yourself the following questions to get to the root of why you're having a hard time letting go of something: If you will not forgive, why? What is your fear? What will you give up if you forgive? What is threatened in your self-understanding, or your understanding of the other person, if you forgive?

If you have decided to forgive, you will notice the decision is not the whole process. It is part of the process. As those memories keep coming up, be sure and breathe through them (belly breathing) and allow them to move on. Don't play the mind games of replaying them, trying to understand every last detail. Let them go.

There is one more part of this forgiveness process, and it is painful. This is where your spouse comes in. Up until now, you could choose to move through the forgiveness process without the participation of your spouse. (You may be including your spouse already by letting them know you are moving through this process, but that is your choice.)

That next part? Apologizing to your spouse.

If you are like most people, every fiber of your body and mind are screaming at me, "That isn't fair, I didn't cheat! Why should I apologize?!"

First, if that is your reaction, you may want to note that you are still attached to the hurt and pain. There is still some forgiving to be done. Keep working the forgiveness process.

Second, remember that role you played in the disconnected relationship? That is where you want to accept accountability. Again, this isn't about blame. It is about responsibility. It is also about changing the process that undermined your marriage.

Recovery after an affair is not about going back to the same old relationship you had. It is about moving to a new relationship – one that is far stronger and healthier than the previous one.

That new relationship requires two people being responsible for themselves and the direction of the marriage. And that can start with accepting your role, then acknowledging it, and finally apologizing to your spouse.

Chapter 7

TRUSTING AFTER INFIDELITY

During infidelity, the person having the affair often minimizes the damage done. That's a human tendency; we tend to compartmentalize things in our lives. We put them in a box, pretending that they have little effect on the other areas of life. But an affair is not just a relationship. It's not just sex. It ruptures one of the core elements of marriage: trust.

There are multiple layers of trust. You can trust your spouse to do what they say they're going to do in daily life. This can be about chores or money or going to work or taking care of the kids. That's just daily trust.

But a deeper trust is about believing somebody will protect the relationship, honoring the vows made when they married. The big one, "forsaking all others," is one of the most powerful protectors of a relationship. It is about keeping other people at arm's length. It is about saving that special relationship for only your spouse. An affair reveals this not to be the case.

Or, to be more clear, it reveals that at a certain point in time, the relationship was not protected.

Does that mean that trust must forever be ruptured?

I don't believe it does. Many people have compared breaking trust to breaking a dish. They believe that once the dish is shattered, even if you glue it back together, it is still fractured. Here's the problem: we humans are not dishes. We are organic. We are designed to heal.

Several years ago, on New Year's Eve, my son tripped at a friend's house and fell off the porch. He broke his arm. He was in horrible pain throughout the night until we could get to a doctor the next day. They x-rayed, and you could easily see the break. The bone had been fractured.

They put it in a temporary cast and sent us to a specialist. The specialist made sure that everything was in the right position, and then covered it with a cast to protect it. The cast, though, was not intended to be a lifetime addition to his arm. It was only there to protect it while the bone healed.

If you were to x-ray his arm today, you might see the scar tissue from the break. You might see the fracture line, but you would also see that the healing was complete. His arm is as good as new, with no residual issues. Yes, you could still locate where the break happened on an x-ray. But it doesn't affect his day-to-day life. In fact, some research shows that bone is actually harder at the point of a fracture once it heals.

Trust is more like a fractured arm than a shattered plate. It can heal and leave no permanent disability. That doesn't mean you won't know it happened; it just means it won't hinder your life.

The Process of Trust

I hear many people talk about "earning trust." That's not really the way trust works. You can act in trustworthy ways, or you can act in untrustworthy ways. But doing so is not about earning trust; it's about being trustworthy.

Trust is a gift. It is always a gift.

At some point, you have to choose to trust someone, to give them the gift of trust. If you don't give them the gift of trust, it will never emerge. As a gift, you have to decide when you will give it. Nobody can make the choice for you. Nobody can force it to happen. It's up to you to decide when to trust.

People can err on either side of the equation when it comes to trust. Sometimes, people make it way too expensive. They choose never to trust again after something traumatic happens, regardless of the situation or circumstances, and regardless of the actions taken by the person who is not being trusted. Sometimes, the trust is held just out of reach. It's used as a weapon against the person trying to earn the trust back. And in some cases, the person has no intention of ever giving the trust again.

In that case, trust is far too expensive.

At the opposite end, there are others who make trust way too cheap. They quickly trust, even when there is evidence that they shouldn't. They choose to trust, even when the person they are trusting continues to violate their trust. This is no better than the "too expensive" trust, as it leaves the trusting person vulnerable to being taken advantage of, and to being hurt. Yet they continue to give away their trust over and over.

Sometimes, right after being hurt, it can feel as if trust can never be rebuilt. It can feel like you need to withhold the trust and make it very expensive. This has more to do with hurt than with trust. As the hurt lessens, it is easier to see a path back to trust. But, that doesn't mean you make it cheap, either.

Trust is a gift — a gift that should be treasured by the person who receives it. Some people act as if it is a cheap gift they can toss aside at any time. Some people haven't even noticed the trust that's been given to them, so they take it for granted.

After infidelity, the person who had the affair realizes they really do want the trust. They want to be given the gift again, to be trusted again, to restore the relationship between them. Many times, people tell me that they are frustrated and angry that their spouse won't trust them. The truth is, trust can be rebuilt — but not in an instant. And not until the hurt has begun to subside, the relationship is in the process of being rebuilt, and clear boundaries have been established to protect the relationship.

In fact, the trust that is ruptured due to an affair, to put it simply, is the type of trust that you will abide by and use to protect the boundaries of the relationship. By protecting the boundaries of the relationship, you will be acting in trustworthy ways. As you act in trustworthy ways, your spouse can begin to see a reason to again give the gift of trust.

Trust is believing that someone has your best interest in mind, or at least the best interest of the relationship, when you are not present. Trust is based on what people do when someone is not watching. It requires a leap of faith, but it is based on watching how you handle small things.

Trust is often given in small increments as the person acts in trustworthy ways with small things. On each side of rebuilding trust, this is important to note. If you are working to trust again, recognize that trustworthiness is seen in pieces. As you give over those pieces, you can see how the other person does. You can begin to assess some characteristics: Is there more connection? Is there more transparency? Are boundaries discussed and set? As that happens, you begin to reestablish trust.

If you are the one working to be trusted, it is important to handle those small pieces as major gifts. Don't treat them as proof that you are not fully trusted. Once you have ruptured trust, it is a process to rebuild it. It is a gift, but given over time. It's kind of like my son's arm healing. The cast went on, but that didn't mean his arm was healed. That only created the protection for his arm as it healed. The healing happened little by little, over the course of the next few months. There was no rushing the healing process. Since the arm was protected, the bones could follow the natural path of healing.

In a marriage, there are really two parts to the trust: Do you trust each other? Do you trust the relationship? The trust in each other is really about having each other's best interest at heart — and actions that demonstrate this. The trust in the relationship is about how it sustains each of your needs for that connection. Will the relationship weather the storms of life's challenges?

Sometimes, people fail to notice these two different levels, lumping everything under "trust." And yet, each is built differently. The first is a type of trust you might have with any important person in your life. Does your boss think of your best interest (or at least consider it)? Does a friend think of your best interest (or at least consider it)? This is the basis for any interaction. We are constantly trying to judge whether there is a place for our own interest — and to what degree we are looking out for the interests of others.

For example, many people feel the sales process (at least, of anything major) has a layer of animosity to it. This is due to the fact that you are constantly judging whether the salesperson is considering your best interest or only their own. Is that car salesman trying to get you what you want, at a fair price, or simply trying to get the biggest addition to their paycheck?

Which brings up an important point in marriage: there are two people invested in the relationship, both with different self-interests. It is a balancing match. Any major decision is a tightrope walk between the interests. Sometimes, the interests match, and a decision is easy. More often, there is not an exact match. The couple must work through those decisions, balancing self-interest with spouse-interest. And likely, someone's interests will be sacrificed.

Trust based on your spouse "always" looking out for your interests is headed for trouble. Trust that you each will do your best to look out for each other's interests is much more reasonable. There will be times when one person's interests will take a secondary position to the other's interests. That's the nature of partnerships. (It should not always be the same person giving in, though. Understand that in major decisions, one or the other will likely give up a little self-interest.)

This is not the layer of trust in which it is helpful to point out, "I trusted you and you ruptured that trust — I will never trust you again." That is more about the relationship.

That layer of trust is really about trusting the relationship and trusting your spouse to protect the relationship. They go hand-in-hand. When a relationship is no longer trusted, it is more likely that someone is not protecting the relationship. When a relationship is disconnected or contentious (or both), a spouse may feel less motivated to protect it. To be clear, this is more about the emotional state of someone rupturing a marriage, not justification for doing so.

The North Star of Commitment

This is an area of strong feeling for me. I truly believe that marriage is protected by commitment. Not by love. Not by passion. Not by happiness. But by commitment. Which is not at all the same as saying that you are bound to a marriage, regardless of emotions or unhappiness. Give me a bit of space to explain. (This is a concept I discuss more fully in my Save the Marriage System, but I'll highlight it here.)

The feeling of love, the passion and attraction, can wax and wane in a relationship. It can feel strong for a period of time, then recede, then return. In fact, most marriages have cycles of feeling more and less connected. Happiness vacillates throughout a person's lifetime, often very independently of the marriage. In fact, I do not believe that marriage was ever meant to be a vehicle for happiness (nor for unhappiness) <find out why in a free training series HERE>.

What guides a marriage is commitment, a promise made. That commitment can guide a couple through some pretty rough waters when it is seen as the North Star of the relationship.

115

Some couples have used false "North Stars," finding themselves adrift in difficult times.

In nautical navigation, ancient mariners could always count on the North Star and use it to find their direction. It was always there (in the Northern Hemisphere). When a storm hit and tossed a ship around, when the storm cleared, there was the North Star to give direction and a reset.

When you marry, you promise to love (not "feel love" but to act in love) each other through good or bad days, sick or healthy days, rich or poor days (doesn't really leave many other days!). And you promised to keep anyone else at a safe distance from the marriage. You also promised to do all of that for the rest of your lives.

That's the commitment.

Some couples base their marriage on love (the feeling). But love (the feeling) will come and go. That's true for every single emotional state. The feeling of passion and the feeling of warmth can sometimes recede in a long-term relationship. (And it can return to that relationship, when you act in ways that move you toward it rather than away from it.) If you base your marriage, though, on the feelings of passion and love, you are "lost at sea" when that goes missing. That is a false North Star.

Some couples base their marriage on happiness. They believe their marriage should bring them happiness and keep them happy. As I noted above, that is not what marriage is for. Happiness is another one of those emotional states that will come and go. Many times, it seems to "go" more than "come" throughout stages of life. But if you base your marriage on

"Happily ever after," you are lost when the "happy" goes on break!

Some couples base their marriage on having wealth or great sex or having fun together. And when that isn't a part of life for one reason or another (even if temporary), then the marriage is lost.

Commitment is the North Star because you get to choose it, honor it, and work within it. When you follow the commitment and work toward it, generally the other pieces fall into place.

Does that mean you just stay in a marriage because of commitment? No. You make the marriage great because you committed to it. The commitment is not all there is. It just gives the foundation to hold you together through the difficult times. And I'm guessing these have been some difficult times.

Let the commitment guide you through; part of that commitment is to build a great marriage.

Trust is part of that great marriage — even when it must be rebuilt. Commitment gives you the reason why you should move toward it and how to move toward it.

Tasks of Trust

Trust should never be given blindly. It should be carefully tested. As a layer of trust is built, another layer can be built on top of it. It's like building a house. You don't start with the roof. You don't start with the rooms. You start with the foundation. The foundation has to be solid, able to support the weight of everything else. In fact, sometimes, after building a foundation, you will see the work crew push against the foundation, jump on it, and make sure it's solid.

Building trust isn't any different. Small tasks taken seriously build the foundation. Then bigger things are shared. As each level goes up, more trust is built. Conversely, if a small task is not honored, it casts doubt on the whole foundation.

So as we have discussed already, trust is a gift. At some point, the person who is going to trust must decide to trust. But that is not something done blindly. It is done based on the fact that the other person is holding up their end of the trust bargain. To be trusted means to be acting trustworthily. Many times, I've heard a spouse ask "Don't you trust me?" Often, that spouse doesn't want to acknowledge the times when he or she has not acted in trustworthy ways.

Trust is a two-way street: one person does trustworthy actions, the other person trusts. It requires both.

Which is why there are "tasks of trust." These are actions that help build trust, or destroy trust if they are not done. They are simple to define: doing the things you say you will do. Those are the tasks of trust. As I discussed earlier, there are different levels of trust. But we humans tend to not do a good job of discerning between the different levels. We look at trust as a single unit. When somebody acts in an untrustworthy way in one area, we apply it to all areas.

This is especially true when there has been infidelity. The foundational commitment has been ruptured, and so all trust is doubted. Which means that if you are trying to rebuild trust, you have to follow through on even the easiest tasks. You have to make sure that you're doing what you say you will do, even in the little things.

Failure to follow through on the small things will lead to more mistrust, tearing down what you are trying to build.

So, if you are trying to build trust, be sure that you take all commitments seriously, even the small ones. And, especially the big ones. If you want to build trust, recognize that the "trust house" has been torn down to its foundations. You're starting over, and someone is testing that foundation. Accept that as the starting point. Take on building trust as a challenge, rebuilding it block-by-block, task-by-task.

If you are the one trying to trust again, recognize that nobody follows through on everything. Your spouse will fall short on some small tasks. Be sure you keep that in mind and don't confuse it with the big trust. At the same time, if you see a pattern of acting in untrustworthy ways, it would be foolish to overlook it and trust immediately. It would be wise to address it directly and clearly.

This is one of the topics that you can cover in your weekly partnership meeting (we'll talk about this more in a later chapter) when you discuss how you are doing. You might note the places where you have a struggle building trust, and why you have that struggle. Be specific about the actions you have seen which have not been completed. Don't assume your spouse knows what's missing. In daily life, some of the things important to one person are less important to the other person. It's easy for somebody to forget something that seems insignificant, not realizing how significant it is to the other person.

A different layer to this is the boundaries of the relationship. Remember, the boundaries are intended to protect the relationship. They also help to build trust. When a spouse sees their partner protecting the relationship, it is easier to trust. When a spouse sees their partner pushing the edges of the boundaries, it raises doubt. One clear way of helping to rebuild trust is to honor and protect the boundaries of the relationship that you and your spouse make. This is especially true after infidelity.

Trust Wrap-Up

There are two parts to the "dance" of trust: acting in trustworthy ways and trusting. Building trust requires both, from each person at the same time. To build trust in a relationship, you have to act trustworthily and give trust. It is a two-way process.

Be realistic about what is necessary to build trust. A spouse forgetting to take out the trash is not part of the deeper trust that we are talking about here. Trusting a spouse to take care of the daily activities is different than trusting a spouse to protect the relationship. Be sure to focus on the important tasks of trust. Don't confuse them with the smaller tasks. It's not that they aren't important; they aren't the game-changers, though, of a relationship.

If you are the spouse who committed infidelity, be patient with building trust. Infidelity is a major blow to trust. It will take some time to rebuild. It can be done, and you will need to be patient while doing it.

If you are the spouse who suffered infidelity, be willing to trust. Let your spouse earn back your trust (even as you continue to act in trustworthy ways). Don't make it too expensive. That causes a great deal of damage to your relationship. If somebody feels that they cannot earn back trust, they will eventually give up. But don't make it too cheap. Trust is a valuable gift. Decide you can rebuild it, and decide you will rebuild it.

Chapter 8

REBUILDING YOUR MARRIAGE

In this chapter, we discuss some strategies for both of you to work on your relationship. Earlier in the book, I devoted one chapter to each of you on what you need to do to address the affair. This chapter is for both of you, to address your marriage.

I want to be as practical as possible in this chapter as we discuss the process of rebuilding your relationship after an affair. My advice will be straightforward, but that doesn't mean it will be easy. As we have already discussed, one of the reasons for the affair is the breakdown of the relationship previously. Therefore, we need to rebuild the relationship.

Very quickly, let me remind you of two elements that were likely not where they should be: connection and boundaries. Likely, as a couple, you were not as emotionally, spiritually, and physically connected as you could have been and needed to be. Likely, boundaries were not in place to keep the relationship safe when the connection waned. It is possible that the two of you had already discussed boundaries, but one chose not to enforce them. It's more likely, as is true for most couples, it never occurred to you to discuss the boundaries.

We also have the issue of reestablishing trust. In fact, this is the trifecta of restoring a relationship after an affair: Rebuilding connection. Clarifying boundaries. Restoring trust.

At this point, it is possible that both of you are wondering whether or not to save the relationship. I work from the assumption that you are going to choose to save your relationship. However, I don't make the assumption at this point that you feel like saving your relationship.

This raises the difference between deciding to do something and feeling like doing it. It is a substantial roadblock for many people. We live in a world that assumes if you don't feel like doing something, you don't have to. At least, we apply this in many areas. In other areas, we know better. For example, you may wake up every day and not feel like going to work, but you likely go to work anyway. Or, you may not always feel like dealing with the kids, yet when there's an issue, you deal with it.

Sometimes, we choose to do things we don't feel like doing because we know it's the right thing to do, the good thing to do, or just what we need to do. Your reasons for saving your marriage after an affair can vary greatly. At this point in your marriage, it is important to know the reasons why you are choosing to save the relationship.

Your Reasons Why

The first assignment for both of you: make a list of all of the reasons why you want to save your relationship. Don't stop at three or four; keep writing. Come up with at least 10 reasons. It may take some time. Don't worry, I'll be waiting right here for you. Just pull out a piece of paper and start brainstorming (and no sharing ideas).

After you have them written down, read through them again; you'll notice some of the "reasons why" are based on fear. For example, you might have a statement about wanting to save the relationship because of the financial devastation a divorce could cause. Notice that while this is a valid reason, it is based on fear.

You might have a reason such as "living out the commitment you made," because you have decided to honor the vows each of you made when you got married. This is about honoring commitment. It is not based on fear.

Those are two very different reasons why you might want to save your relationship. So, once more, read through them again. This time, mark out all of the fear-based reasons.

You now have deeper reasons to save your relationship. These reasons are important because the fear-based reasons, over time, will lose their energy. We get used to things that scare us, and they just fall into the background. They no longer help us move forward and no longer work as reasons to stay in the relationship.

But those deeper reasons, those more purposeful reasons, are your true "reasons why." They will pull you through the more difficult days. (And there will be difficult days.) This recovery process is not a long slow climb, always getting better, with the relationship improving daily. Instead, it is an up and down path through the mountains and dark valleys.

If you have ever been through physical therapy for an injury, you may remember healing often comes with a bit of pain and discomfort. That is not an indication you are doing something wrong or that even trying is wrong. Only that healing can be uncomfortable.

There may be days you doubt what you are doing, when others doubt what you are doing, and when you're ready to quit. Always remember those deeper reasons why; pull out your list every now and then, just to keep in mind what you're doing and why you're doing it. Those deeper reasons provide you with inspiration and determination when you are lagging internally. Write down that list of "Why's" and keep it nearby for each of you.

Let's be very clear that our task here is not to get you back to where you were, but to create a new place to be. The old relationship did not get you where you needed to be. The old relationship brought you here. It won't get you to the new place.

That could be a bit worrisome to you, as you don't know what the new path is or where it's going. But what we are trying to build is a loving, supportive relationship, based on commitment. We are creating a team, or as I refer to it, a WE. (I discuss this concept in-depth in my Save the Marriage System.)

Basically, a WE is a relationship where you both feel that you have each other's back, that you're working towards a common direction, that the connection has been nurtured, that you both make decisions based on what is best for the relationship, and that you both willingly protect the relationship.

Are you ready to sign up for that? If so, that's what we're working on.

Your Vision for Your Marriage

Let's now create a vision for what you want in your relationship, a vision statement for your marriage. For many years, companies have made a practice of creating a vision statement for their businesses. This vision statement is not about how they do things, but where they are trying to get to, and why they want to get there. The vision statement is an aspirational statement that guides the company towards its mission.

A corporation and a marriage share some things in common. In the beginning, both are just concepts; entities that are created in imagination, and become real in execution. A corporation is a legal entity. When it is treated as something real, and when people are moving in the same direction, it becomes real. A marriage is a legal entity. In the beginning, it only exists in imagination. As both people treat it with respect, as both people honor the boundaries of the relationship, as both people work on connection, it becomes more and more real.

Vision statements give corporations clarity in their direction and values. And a vision statement can do the same for your marriage.

At this point, you may be much more clear about what you don't want. You likely don't want any more secrecy, any more broken boundaries, any more hurt and pain from betrayal. You probably don't want any more distance.

But knowing what you don't want doesn't get you very far. It may tell you what to avoid, but gives you little direction about where to head. Direction only comes from knowing what you want, and pointing in that direction.

So what DO you want? This is the purpose of the vision statement of your marriage. The vision statement will point you toward what you want, and how you want to get there. Remember, this is YOUR vision statement. It is not a statement of what you think others want for you, or what they think a marriage should be. It is what you want in your marriage. It's not about what it "should be," but about what it "could be." And more importantly, the statement is what it "will be," as you head in that direction.

A major mistake people make, when they are working on their vision statement, is they make it too difficult. They want it to be literary and poetic. They imagine it in big script calligraphy, a beautiful, framed statement. If that is what comes to mind, drop that thought. We want a practical statement. We want a useful statement. We want the statement that will help you move in a better direction. Don't complicate it. (And if you choose to have it made into a framed calligraphic picture, you can always choose to do so later.)

You don't have a committee, like a corporation might have, as you are writing this. You have the two of you. It is a combination of working alone and bringing it together. So, consider yourself a committee of two – the only two who matter.

Homework for Each of You

Each of you will want to spend some time thinking about what you want in the relationship. Individually, you each will write a version of your vision statement. This is not THE vision statement, the one that will guide your relationship. It is just thinking about the vision statement. In other words, in some ways, it is your side of the potential vision statement. Not everything you want may make it into the final draft. But the final draft should represent something that matches for both of you.

Here are some rules to think about as you compose your vision statement:

1. Vision statements are aspirational, moving you toward something. They are not about avoiding something. Don't use the vision statement as a way of stating what you don't want.

2. Your statement, and the statement you come up with together, should evoke an emotional response. If you read the statement and feel nothing, it provides no vision and no aspiration. Start over.

3. A vision statement is not about what a person "should do." It is a relational statement, about where the relationship could go. It is more about the relationship than the individuals. The statement guides each of you on how to get to the relationship you want. It is about the possible, assuming each of you moves in that direction.

4. A vision statement is not a contract. Don't try to enforce it. It is something to move towards. When we try to enforce such things, it becomes about our own fear.

5. A vision statement is not a weapon. You don't pull it out during a conflict, to hold it over the other person. You don't make threats with it. Vision statements hold more weight in times of peace and effort than in times of conflict. If you are following your vision statement, moving in that direction during the good times, it will impact the relationship in times of conflict.

With those thoughts in mind, each of you can write a vision statement for the relationship. Vision statements do not need to go on for pages and pages. They are not an opportunity to score points (or make a point) or to shame a spouse. This is not the time to try to point out where your spouse has fallen short or make an argument.

This is a chance to begin moving towards the relationship each of you wants.

There are no defined formulas for writing the statement. In fact, I won't even provide you with a template. This is a creative process. And it needs to reflect you.

At this point, you may be feeling like this is going to be a difficult process. It's not. That's just your mind fooling you into looking for an easy way out. It will take a little bit of time, and a little bit of effort, but it will be YOUR statement.

Make a deadline with each other on when you will come back together to share your vision statement. Don't wait for this to just happen. Give yourselves a couple of days, and schedule a time to sit down together. People are people and tend to procrastinate where they can. Without a deadline, it probably won't happen. (And by the way, procrastination is not necessarily a sign of resistance, an indication of lack of care, or any other assumption you may make about the procrastinator. It's just human nature.)

When you sit down together, read your vision statement to each other. In fact, read it to each other a couple of times.

Make a list of all of the common points you have on your statements. Sometimes, couples who have been in conflict do not believe they will have common parts. Those couples tend to surprise themselves with how much they have in common. Most people want very similar things out of a relationship. They may not know how to get there, but they often want the same things.

Make a list of the common points. Make another list of the different points.

For each of the different points, discuss why you wrote what you wrote. Discuss what it means, and why it is important to you. Sometimes, each person comes up with points that didn't occur to the other person, but to which that person also agrees (and it doesn't mean anything that they didn't come up with it, so don't read into that). If that is the case, you and your spouse may choose to move it to the list of common points you made. If you can't agree on it, leave it on the different points list.

Set that aside for a day, and then return to it. See if there has been any shift, either way, about the list of different points. You may find that the heart of the matter in those differences is already covered in the points you agree to. You may find that some of the points on the "different" list are irrelevant because of things on the list of common points.

There may be some points on which you both cannot agree. I suggest you leave them off. Many times, people start arguing to get their point included, but from a more objective viewpoint, this isn't important. You are not trying to get your way, you are creating a vision statement of a relationship to which you both aspire.

Now that you have your list of elements for your vision statement, as a couple, write it together. Use short, descriptive paragraphs. You can elaborate on points for clarity. Again, there's no template for this, as it should reflect what both of you feel about the relationship. It needs to be in your own words.

There is no right or wrong length, only a length which covers what you want. Some people can encapsulate this in just a couple of paragraphs. Other people have vision statements that go on for pages. It's up to you. Just make sure the vision statement reflects what both of you want out of the relationship as you move forward.

Speaking Each Other's Language

One of my favorite relationship concepts is the idea of love languages. Gary Chapman introduced this idea, and it has transformed many couples. Gary says that each of us has a certain language for how we hear love. We speak love from that same language – which is why couples get into trouble. Many times, our primary language of love is not the same as our spouse's language of love. So we misunderstand the love our spouse is speaking to us. We might not just misunderstand – we may not even hear it!

In the beginning of a relationship, most people are speaking every possible language, trying to win over someone. This makes it confusing later on, because when life returns to normal, we start using only our primary language (at least most of the time). So, the other person can miss the love coming their way. And vice versa.

In his book, The Five Love Languages, Chapman notes the five primary love languages people speak: Quality Time, Words of Affirmation, Touch, Gifts, and Acts of Service.

There is no right or wrong love language, only different ones. To follow the analogy, it's kind of like all of the languages in the world. No one language is right or wrong. Each is just a way of expressing thoughts and ideas. But if you don't know the language or how to speak it, everything gets lost in translation.

The task is to learn to speak your spouse's love language and hear your spouse's love language as it is spoken to you. In strong relationships, both people are trying to speak the other person's love language.

If you don't know your love language (or you don't know your spouse's), Dr. Chapman has a free test on his website. Let me suggest that both of you take this test so that you know the love language of the other person. You don't have to be an expert in all the languages to grasp this concept. You just want to start speaking your spouse's love language.

Here's why this is so important: many times, I see people who desperately love their spouse, but their spouse doesn't feel it. Over time, the feeling of connection begins to wane. Both people feel unwanted. The connection begins to fail, not because of a lack of love, but a lack of hearing the love. What a tragedy when the love is there, but can't be heard.

Which is why, in the process of connecting with each other, it is important to make sure that you are speaking your spouse's love language, on both sides.

The good thing about love languages is that they are much easier to learn than a foreign language. Trust me on that! (I have managed to study and fail at learning five foreign languages, but I do grasp love languages!)

Once you have learned each other's love language, the translation begins to go both ways. Each of you will be able to see the love coming toward you from your spouse. And you will also be able to show love to your spouse in the language that speaks most deeply to him or her.

Many times, the adjustment is fairly minor. It is not about starting to show love, but about showing love in a way that makes the most impact on your spouse. And we all want our spouses to feel the love we show, right?

Levels of Connection

There are three types or levels of connection: physical, emotional, and spiritual. Working on the connection in each of these areas is important. Many couples have lost touch in one or all levels, and some couples never make it past two of the levels. But once you understand the levels, it is easy to rebuild them.

First, let's talk about why this connection is so important. Humans are wired for connection, as we discussed earlier. If the connection is not there, it can become very painful. In fact, researchers have noted that the hurt of disconnection is actually felt physically.

In other words, the need to connect is so deep that it's not just in our heads; the need is also in our body. Many living creatures in the world share our need for connecting. It's what creates herds and tribes. But the depth of connection in a marriage is uniquely human.

Physical connection is something we share with those other creatures. And to some degree, emotional connection is also something we share. But humans share an emotional connection through words, not just presence. And we uniquely share our spiritual connection.

Three levels of connection: Physical, Emotional, and Spiritual. When they are working, they create incredibly strong relationships. When they are missing, they create incredibly painful relationships.

In my book, *How to Save Your Marriage in Three Simple Steps*, I go into detail about how to connect in all three areas. But I want to spend some time doing the same here so you can begin to build your connection together.

Physical Connection

Physical connection is not just about sex. Physical connection is any contact between two people, body to body. Skin is the largest of the organs in your body; it covers your entire body, a barrier and a connection to the external world. It triggers hormonal responses when it is touched and is the transmitter of physical connection.

For example, when you hug somebody for more than just a few seconds, your body releases oxytocin into your bloodstream. This is a bonding hormone, created by touch on the skin. It bonds babies with their parents, and it bonds couples to each other. (And it's part of the bonding that happens with any prolonged contact – one of the dangers of inappropriate physical contact outside of marriage.)

Simply stated, physical connection happens when there is physical contact. A touch, a hug, holding hands, kissing, caressing, body massages, and sex. All are physical connection, at least as long as the connection is desired. If forced, any of these connections are quite the opposite, violations to the individual and breaking connection.

In a marriage, loving touch creates physical connection, especially when both people are on board with the connection. At our most core, basic level, physical connection is created in touch. It is primal enough that it often happens automatically.

As you work to recover your relationship, you may find that you have gotten out of the habit of being physically connected. You may have stopped touching each other, or only touch each other during sex. This is your chance to begin to reestablish a full connection of touch. But, you may be breaking or changing habits. Accept that it may take a little bit of time to get used to this. If you are out of the habit, it can feel foreign and uncomfortable.

How do you get beyond the awkwardness of any activity? Continuing to do it. Start small, and build up. Touches on the arms and shoulders are usually safer then touches on the upper legs or torso.

For right now, have a discussion about what feels comfortable, recognizing that the "comfort" should be a little bit uncomfortable. You should be stretching a little bit. Remember, you're building new habits. If you have disconnected physically, it won't feel like it comes naturally.

But let me also remind you that this is very similar to what happens at the beginning of a relationship. You were probably fairly awkward as you began touching each other in those early days. You probably quickly adapted (and may not even remember it). Unless you overthink this, you will now, too.

Since you are reestablishing this, it is okay to talk about touching. Yes, I know you may think it should "just happen." But it rarely works that way. Most people don't "just happen" to start eating well or exercising or any other habit. Most people don't "just happen" to master a skill without practice and intentionality. Let go of the myth and see that what you are doing is building something important. Don't let the discomfort keep you from moving forward with connecting.

Emotional Connection

Emotional connection is the sense of somebody being there, on your side. Emotional connection usually happens in dialogue and conversation. That doesn't mean the connection is only vocal. For example, if you are sharing something difficult and painful, it can feel connecting if the other person sits with you quietly, but is clearly interested in listening. Contrast that with telling somebody something important, while they are looking down at a phone or up at a TV. One way feels like connecting, and the other way feels like distancing.

In the midst of tough times, presence may be all that is necessary. Sitting with each other through tough times is emotional connection. Talking with each other about your emotional life is emotional connection. Giving supportive responses or looks are both emotional connection.

Some things get in the way of emotional connection. Hurt, anger, resentment, frustration, and other negative emotions can lead to a lack of emotional connection. Here's the irony: connection helps to heal the negative emotions between you. This is not a chicken–or–egg issue. You don't have direct control over the emotions, but you do have a choice about your actions.

You can choose to work toward emotional connection – not because you feel it, but because you want to build it. You can choose to build the connection, not just wait for it to emerge.

Which circles us back to the need for forgiveness, and brings us to the realization that we can always choose to connect, even when there is some distance between us. In fact, connection grows on itself. The more you work on the connection, the more the connection grows which leads to more work on the connection which leads to more growth of connection. But you must choose to get started.

Why is forgiveness important here? Because it frees up emotional energy that is held back by the resentment. Think of those negative emotions as dams for connection. When you remove the dams, the connection flows. As the connection flows, it can also destroy the dams. A good starting point, though, is forgiveness. It is a process you can choose at any time. (And, as a reminder, the forgiveness is for the person forgiving – a choice that can be made at any time.)

Emotional connection includes listening to the other person, responding empathetically, sitting with the other person as they discuss their day, and providing support in tough times. If you find yourself to be someone who doesn't have the right words to say, remember that sometimes just sitting there quietly and saying, "I'm so sorry, I'm here for you," is enough during tough times.

When we are emotionally connected with somebody, we're not just listening to the facts they are telling us, but to the emotions behind them. We are responding to how they're feeling, not just what they are saying. And we get better with practice.

There is a common confusion for some people that when a person is telling us about a tough situation, what they want is for us to fix it. Sometimes (and perhaps most of the time), they just want support, to know it was tough and they are supported.

Notice the difference between two responses to: "I just left the worst meeting with my boss! It seems that she has it out for me! Nothing I said was right. Everything was challenged. I've had it."

Response #1: "You can't let that happen! You should: (a) Go beg her to keep you on board, since we need the job! (b) Complain to HR! I think she is biased. (c) Quit. You don't have to take that! (d) Write her a letter and try to explain." (First, note that any one of these may be correct. But second, all are trying to solve it.)

Response #2: "Wow! That sounds like a rough day! I'm sorry it was a tough meeting. Tell me what happened." No fixing. No pushing or suggesting. Just an acknowledgment that it was tough and you are supporting.

Once you break the need to fix, you realize that emotional support is actually much easier. It is being present and on the side of your spouse. And your spouse may eventually ask, "What do you think I should do?" (By the way, the answer is not, "You should . . ." but, "I think you should/could/might consider . . . .")

Emotional connection is often silent but present. If you are looking at a beautiful or horrific scene, side-by-side, near each other, that can be emotionally connecting. If words are needed, that can be connecting. The biggest shift: knowing you are on each other's side.

Spiritual Connection

Spiritual connection is a level of connection that many couples miss. It is a deeper level of sharing, and not something we do with too many people. Spiritual connection is talking about what really matters to you. Don't confuse it with religious discussions (although they can be included here, as long as they are not debates, just sharing). When we talk about what is meaningful to us: our purpose in life, where we want to get to, our dreams and aspirations, and our beliefs, we are sharing a spiritual connection. If you are like most people, you know how rare that level of sharing is in your own life.

In fact, many couples share very little spiritual connection. Many people don't think to talk about these areas, and others are self-conscious about discussing them. Again, with some practice, it gets easier. Most of us have been trained to avoid such areas. And while you might not want to share such things at a cocktail party, it is a great way to build a connection with your spouse. It is also an excellent way of building a life that hits on your deeper meaning and purpose.

Usually, we only share that type of information with the most important people in our lives. You are entrusting each other with the deepest levels of thoughts and feelings. It is a level of vulnerability that many people never achieve.

One caveat here: you must be clear about your dreams and aspirations. You need to have thought through what you believe. You need to be working on your life purpose, finding your life meaning. You can't share these areas until you have at least begun thinking through them. You don't have to have the answers. The sharing can be about your questions. But questions (and answers) don't come without some focus on those areas.

And yes, you will feel self-conscious in both saying and listening to these deep areas. But don't miss the opportunity to learn about each other at these deepest levels. There is only one way to connect in such a way: risk the sharing.

When a relationship is strained, any or all of these areas may be suffering. You may have cut off the physical connection long ago, provide very little emotional connection with each other, and may have never shared a spiritual connection.

But guess what? That can change whenever you want. You can deliberately choose to move towards connection with your spouse in all three areas. As you work on this together, talk about the connection. In fact, you can talk about all three connections. But let me suggest that the conversations be about how to grow, not why it's not there. In other words, don't come at it from the negative. Move from the aspirational:

"How would you like to build a connection?"

"What would you like in a physical connection?"

"What would you like in an emotional connection?"

"What would you like in a spiritual connection?"

At a tender point in the relationship, it is usually not helpful to criticize what is not there or cast blame for the disconnection. It is more helpful to build toward something that you do want, rather than critiquing what you don't want.

We humans have a tendency for being critical, and that often traps us in a loop. Instead of moving towards "how," we move towards "why." That is rarely a helpful conversation.

"How" is a building discussion: "How do we build more connection in our marriage?"

"Why" is a trapping discussion: "Why don't we have more connection in our marriage?"

One opens possibilities, and the other creates an endless loop. Which one do you want to be stuck in?

The Partnership Meeting

Let me suggest a simple model for meeting together that can be very beneficial for rebuilding the relationship. This is a suggestion I make to people who are rebuilding their relationship, and to people who want to improve their relationship.

I call it the Partnership Meeting. Think of it in terms of a business meeting. Remember, this is just an analogy. I'm not suggesting that you treat your marriage like a business.

Most businesses have business meetings, and partnerships have partnership meetings. They are ways to stay on track and assure you're moving in the right direction. It's important for the members of any entity to be on board with the direction.

(The reason I use the business analogy is because corporations and marriages both start as imaginary entities, and only become real when we treat them as real. The purpose of a business is to make a profit. The purpose of a marriage and family is to create love. So they have different goals, but a similar underlying construction.)

A partnership meeting should be held on a regular basis. I recommend weekly. And I also recommend you choose a set time and location. Treat it as an important meeting. If others ask you to schedule something at the same time, simply tell them you have a prior commitment already. This is a good way of modeling how to protect the relationship anyway, and it establishes a meeting that is shared between the two of you. If you had an important meeting at work, you probably would not schedule over it. Treat this the same way.

A partnership meeting requires both of you to show up, ready to go. There is no secretary, no keeper. Both of you are responsible for keeping your own notes. Both of you are responsible for the meeting. There is no leader or convener.

If you decide to be responsible for something, make your own notes about it, remind yourself about it, and take responsibility for it. This is an equal partnership, and the meeting should represent that.

There are three "orders of business" in the partnership meeting: schedule, finances, and connection.

During day-to-day life, many couples get stuck in petty arguments over scheduling issues. Perhaps it is about where the kids are, or where either of you are. But somehow, scheduling creates unnecessary conflict for many couples, usually because they don't have a set time to talk about the schedule and make sure they are both on the same page. Here is your opportunity.

In the scheduling, it is simply a matter of having your calendars out and making sure you each know what's on the family calendar and on your individual calendars. Coordinate any issues of scheduling at this time. It may not take very long, but for many families, it can be complicated. Coordinating schedules rarely happens at the end of a busy day; use the meeting to get it off the plate, covered, and set aside.

The financial segment of the meeting is to keep both people on the same page about the family finances. This can cover the immediate financial issues as well as any financial issues on the horizon. In many families, one person is responsible for balancing the checkbook and paying the bills. Sometimes, that leads to the other person being in the dark on those issues. Likewise, in many families, one person takes the lead in dealing with any investments or savings, and sometimes that leads to the other person being in the dark on those issues.

So, the financial segment is designed to remove the chance of conflict that comes from a lack of awareness. The goal is to make sure everything is jointly known and to build a WE around money. This creates some very healthy couple habits. Both people need to be aware of the money situation, and any potential crises on the horizon. (Remember, money is listed as the number one issue when people discuss why they get divorced.)

Again, this is not the time to iron out all the details and take all the actions. It is the time to update each other on any issues that may be looming, and make a decision as to who is going to follow up on those issues. Partnership meetings are about moving forward and solving issues. If you realize that there is an issue with money, one person can choose to find a solution, reporting back the next time. Solve the issue by finding a solution, rather than spending endless iterations discussing the problem.

The third section is about connection. This is not therapy without a therapist. This is not your chance to ambush your spouse about where your spouse is falling short. This is a chance for both of you to check in on how you're doing.

You start this conversation with the simple question, "How are we doing?" Remember, this is not a chance to complain, to argue, or to "therapize" with your spouse. It is an opportunity to check in and see how each of you feels about the connection between you.

(CAUTION: Do not start with "How are YOU doing?" That leads to a conversation about the interior emotional life of the individuals. This is about "how WE are doing as a couple." Small difference in words; big difference in outcome.)

One person may say, "I'm not feeling as connected as I would like." From there, it is not about answering "why" the connection is not working, but to think about "how" you could fix the connection. A good response to hearing your spouse is not connected would be to ask, "What could we do to help with the connection?" In other words, look for a solution.

On a daily basis, many couples get caught in this "why" question, rather than looking for a solution to it. We have come to believe that if you can find the "why" you automatically have the solution. But almost always, the question of "why" keeps you stuck in a loop of trying to figure things out, without ever getting to the action. Connection never comes from wondering, it always comes from action.

At this point in your partnership meeting, you have coordinated your schedule, discussed any outstanding financial issues, expressed the level of connection or disconnection in your relationship, and perhaps even decided upon some actions each of you need to take. If there are action steps, each of you is responsible for the actions you agree to. It is not up to either spouse to keep checking to see if the other takes action. When you meet again (the following week), be sure to have your notes about your actions, your solutions, and any other steps. And remember, this is a partnership. Treat the meeting like a partnership. Both are responsible, both show up, and both take action.

How to Connect in One Word

If you want to connect, how to do it can be summed up in one word: Connect. Practice the connection. Put it into action. Be with each other on a physical, emotional, and spiritual plane.

Humans are natural connectors. We just let "stuff" (a kinder word than I might otherwise use) get in the way. Hurt, anger, resentment – they all cloud out connection. But hurt can heal. Hurtful actions can be forgiven. That helps to clear some of that stuff.

Choosing to Show Up (learn more in the free training HERE) can help each of you to bring your presence back into the relationship. In fact, if you don't show up, you aren't offering much for your spouse to connect to. Notice, though, that showing up is a choice. Make that choice.

Connection is simple: Connect. Notice I said "simple," not "easy." Especially after the confusion of an affair. It is confusing because of the feelings involved for the people in the affair. The excitement and adrenaline can feel good, especially when compared to a disconnected and hurting marriage. But "feeling good" is not the same as "good and healthy." Still, it leads to confusion for the spouse who had the affair.

And often, when a spouse breaks an affair and returns to the marriage, the spouse carries shame from their infidelity. Often, in retrospect, as the justifications fall, shame and guilt enter. This is normal; most people, in less confused spots, do not find affairs to be in their moral keeping.

Self-forgiveness is as important as forgiving another person. We, humans, tend to make some fairly unhealthy choices with our emotional brain, and then justify it with our reasoning brain. But as the emotional brain returns to normal, those "reasons" tend to fall apart, leaving humans with "I don't know why I did that." This can be tough on both spouses.

It is also a normal part of the way our brain works. Like it or not, we are far less rational than we like to believe.

For the spouse who suffered the affair, it can be equally confusing. The trust you had in the relationship has been ruptured. You may also be searching for the "reasons why," frustrated that there aren't any clear answers. Remember, the human brain makes emotional decisions and then rationalizes them. As emotions shift, the rationalizations fall apart, leaving confusion.

That sense of betrayal, the hurt that comes from it, and the anger that erupts from the hurt are normal. Those all will begin to abate over time.

But you both need to understand one crucial point: you never will go back to where you were before the affair. The relationship has forever been changed.

Notice that I did not say "changed for the worse." Just changed. Many couples come out of an affair with a stronger, more durable relationship. That is your aim.

You may choose a relationship that is more:

- Connected
- Protected
- Intentional
- Honest
- Realistic
- Shared
- Mutual

The path back? It's connection. It is rebuilding the connection and the boundaries. Staying in touch with each other. Refusing to take the relationship for granted.

While we humans are pretty good at making things complicated, many times, the answer is surprisingly simple. But never confuse "simple" with "easy."

I've noticed many times when I suggest people work on the connection I get an immediate response of "I don't know how." But you do. Connecting is in our biology, our genetic makeup. We start connecting with others at birth and don't stop until we die. Every day, you connect with people.

So why, at this point, do people say, "I don't know how"? Often, it is the hurt and frustration talking; it is questioning why it didn't work before. More often than not, the connection in a marriage wanes from neglect and hurt. NOT from a lack of knowing how.

If you need further resources, let me point to a few I have mentioned:

How to Save Your Marriage in 3 Simple Steps

The 5 Love Languages

Save the Marriage System

Those resources will give you information to help you move forward. But each of you must choose to take action.

Conclusion

(STARTING POINT FOR YOU)

——————～——————

Here we are at the end (but only the end of this book). It is the beginning of your process to a strong and thriving marriage. Congratulations on making the decision to recover your marriage. While you cannot predict exactly where you are headed, making that choice opens up possibilities in your relationship that were not there before.

A central truth of being human is the fact that when things are rough, it can feel like we are the only ones having to deal with it. It is also true at such times that many other people are going through the same thing. This is certainly true with infidelity. It happens in many marriages. Sometimes, couples decide they cannot work through this issue.

However, many times couples emerge from such an incident with a stronger relationship. But let me be entirely honest: Some people bail at the very beginning, seeing no alternative to ending the marriage. Some people decide at some point in the process they simply cannot move forward. Many people do work through the process, rebuilding and re-establishing their relationship – re-creating their marriage. It is impossible to know which category your relationship will be in until you do the work.

I have worked with people who swore at some point in life, that if there were ever infidelity in a relationship, that relationship would end. I watched as they rebuilt their marriage. I worked with people who swore that they would stay together through anything, only to realize that they could not stay together through infidelity. Whatever you believed at the outset of your relationship, it's been challenged and redefined along the way.

The decision to work on the marriage or end the marriage is a deeply personal decision. It takes two votes to continue the marriage. It only requires one vote to end it. That vote is for each of you to decide. My suggestion is to work on rebuilding. Go through the steps I've outlined, work on the issues you've uncovered, and see if you can rebuild.

I've seen it enough times to know that it is entirely possible to rebuild your marriage. That is something you may not be able to see from your current perspective – which is why I want to assure you, it is absolutely possible, and it can absolutely happen. But I didn't say it would be painless or easy.

These are issues that need to be resolved, regardless of the outcome of the relationship. If you are like most couples, you probably have children. Given that, you are linked together for the rest of your lives. Problems and issues in the relationship will continue to show themselves until they are resolved. So why not work to resolve them, and see if the relationship can be rebuilt?

If you are still reading at this point, I have to believe you are moving in that direction, too. So, if you haven't already, it's time to get started.

We've covered the reasons that affairs happen: lack of connection and lack of boundaries. We've covered the fuel that makes affairs burned so hot: adrenaline attraction. We've examined why sex is such an issue in our lives and in our marriages: deep connection and acceptance. We've laid out a process for forgiveness, steps to take in an ongoing process. We've discussed what each person needs to do in order to work towards recovery, both the person who had the affair and the person who suffered the affair. We've looked at the issue of trust and how to regain that trust. Most importantly, we've examined how to rebuild the marriage.

All words. Until you put them into practice. Then, the words become real. Words are powerful. Your marriage began with words. As you follow those words, they become more real. The shift is from words to action. Many times, people read a book and set it aside. That is not my intent for this book. I don't write to satisfy curiosity or for general interest, but to give you a path. A path that begs to be followed.

It's now up to the two of you to begin walking that path. At the end, you'll find the treasure of a deeply satisfying marriage that each of you will protect, and which will nurture each of you.

Time to head in that direction.

I'm pulling for you!

**As a reader of this book, I want to provide you with an extra bonus I didn't include in the main body. I collected some very common questions that come up for people as they move through this process. Resources are provided for each of you.

Please go here for your bonus:
http://savethemarriage.com/affair-bonus

RESOURCES

I mentioned several resources throughout this book, and wanted to give you some shortcuts to find them. Here is your "cheatsheet" for more help:

Your BONUS Q&A:
http://savethemarriage.com/affair-bonus

No Pause Button In Marriage
http://savethemarriage.com/nopause

Anxiety and Breathing
http://savethemarriage.com/breathe

Show Up Training
http://savethemarriage.com/showup

Immutable Laws Of Marriage Series
http://savethemarriage.com/ilm

Gary Chapman's book, *The 5 Love Languages*
http://savethemarriage.com/5love

My book, *How to Save Your Marriage in Three Simple Steps*
http://savethemarriage.com/book

The Save The Marriage System
http://savethemarriage.com

ABOUT THE AUTHOR

Dr. Lee Baucom is an author, coach, consultant, therapist, and frequent speaker. In his work, Dr. Baucom strives to build even broken and hurting marriages into a relationship to be treasured and protected.

The author of a number of books, including *Thrive Principles* and *How To Save Your Marriage In 3 Simple Steps*, Dr. Baucom provides practical steps to create a thriving life.

If you would like to contact Dr. Baucom for coaching, consulting, or speaking, you can contact him here:

Aspire Coaching

4949 Brownsboro Rd., #147

Louisville, Kentucky 40222

502-802-4823

Lee@SaveTheMarriage.com

Made in the USA
Columbia, SC
16 July 2021